Sm02006254

KT-527-997

JDF
(Gan)

Targets for Tomorrow's Schools

075 070 9499

To Cathy Wood
The better teacher

Change begets change. Nothing propagates so fast.
Charles Dickens: Martin Chuzzlewit

Targets for Tomorrow's Schools

A Guide to Whole School Target-setting for Governors and Headteachers

Nigel Gann

FALMER PRESS
Taylor & Francis Group

UK   Falmer Press, 1 Gunpowder Square, London, EC4A 3DF
USA   Falmer Press, Taylor & Francis Inc., 325 Chestnut Street, 8th Floor,
            Philadelphia, PA 19106

First published in 1999

**A catalogue record for this book is available from the British
Library**

ISBN 0 7507 0949 9

**Library of Congress Cataloging-in-Publication Data are available
on request**

Jacket design by Caroline Archer

Typeset in 10/12pt Garamond by
Graphicraft Limited, Hong Kong

*Printed in Great Britain by Biddles Ltd., Guildford and King's Lynn
on paper which has a specified pH value on final paper manufacture
of not less than 7.5 and is therefore 'acid free'.*

Contents

Contents

List of tables and figures

Tables

Figures

Acknowledgments

I am grateful to the following for permission to reproduce figures:

Sammons, Hillman and Mortimore (1995) for table 2.2 on page 19 from *Key Characteristics of Effective Schools: A Review of School Effectiveness Research*, London: Ofsted.

The DfEE for figure 4.1 (page 47) from *Guidance on Good Governance*.

Woolston Infants School, Southampton for figure 4.2 on page 50.

North Manchester High School for Girls, for figure 8.1 on page 82.

Alan Lawrie for figure 10.1 (page 98) from *Managing Quality of Service*, Directory of Social Change.

Kogan Page for table 10.1 (page 106) from *Total Quality Management in Education*, Sallis (1993) London: Kogan Page.

Preface

I am deeply indebted to a number of people without whom this book would not have been produced. None of us who work with school governing bodies can do so without recognizing an enormous debt to Joan Sallis who, though only a small Welsh woman herself, provides the giant's shoulders on which we all stand.

I am grateful to a number of local education authorities and other organizations, and have drawn heavily upon my work with them for this book. Dorset County Council and its School Improvement Service continue to provide a model for other LEAs in their support of governing bodies — they strike the right balance of letting good governing bodies get on with the job without intruding, while supporting them in difficult times, and offering high quality training and development to all governors. I also thank Cornwall, Somerset, Southwark and Tower Hamlets LEAs. The Community Education Development Centre has taken on some of the supportive and developmental role previously undertaken by AGIT (Action for Governor Information and Training). Their sustenance of those of us who are interested in school governance is indispensible. I am lucky to have as colleagues such people as Paddy O'Brien, David Rees, Martin Corrick, Colin Fletcher and Karen Lynch. They have immeasurably enriched my work.

Anna Clarkson of Falmer Press has continued to show faith in the book. Thanks to her and her team for their support and encouragement.

Once again, the true progenitor of this book is Cathy Wood, who has contributed so much in a career at the chalkface, while inspiring the thinking behind this work.

Thanks finally to the thousands of school governors who have contributed to this book without knowing it. The contribution they make to improving the education service of this country will never be adequately recognized.

Nigel Gann
October 1998

Introduction

What Are Schools For?

What should children do at school? What should children be able to do when they leave? It seems extraordinary that, until comparatively recently, no local or national standards were laid down for either of these two fundamental expectations. In the 1970s, the largest education authority in the country made no demands on schools in terms of the things that happened in them, nor of the things the children might reasonably be expected to be able to do at any stage in their education. Teachers decided these things for themselves. The only restriction on what they taught — and seen by the profession as an almost intolerable constraint — was the examination system, which was dominated by the universities. Even so, it applied to only a minority of children.

But since 1976, there has been a sea-change in the expectations that society has of schools. Two themes have dominated the education debate. Sometimes these have seemed to be complementary. Sometimes, they have seemed in direct contradiction to each other. On the one hand, there has been a requirement for far greater accountability. What should schools be doing with children? What can we expect children to achieve? How well — or how badly — are schools actually performing?

Simultaneously, there has arisen a demand for a greater sense of public ownership of a service owned largely by its own profession — perhaps because such ownership would require, and may even be able itself to bring about, raised standards; perhaps because, as life and the welfare state become ever more complicated and out of our control, we feel a need to reassert our democratic ownership of state institutions.

Accountability and Ownership

The famous speech by Prime Minister James Callaghan at Ruskin College in October 1976 marked a watershed in government attitudes to the content and outcomes of education. Ever since, there has been increasing dictation of the inputs made by schools, both in their nature — through the National Curriculum, through direct funding of initiatives bypassing local education authorities, through examination and assessment, and in their quality — through inspection and the publication of inspection reports, through expected levels of attainment, through the compilation and public dissemination of school results.

At the same time as this growing centralization and 'professionalization' of the schools system, government legislation has brought into play a dimension in school management which was hitherto largely irrelevant — community participation in individual school governance. The history and the impact of this is charted in *Improving School Governance* (Gann, 1998), which was written during the last days of the 18-year Conservative administration and the early months of the Labour government.

The two themes of accountability and ownership came together in the first educational legislation of the new Parliament, in 1997 and 1998. The increasing rigour demanded of schools is expressed in the government's requirement that all schools set targets for pupil performance (DfEE, 1998b). The public ownership of schools is reinforced by the fact that these targets will be set and monitored by the school governing body, that unique combination of professional and lay people which carries the ultimate responsibility for what goes on in schools. The governing bodies, regenerated by the 1986 and 1988 Education Acts, reflect our membership, in the early days of the third millennium, of an imperfect but aspirational 'representative' government — what Aneurin Bevan called approvingly 'the government of the experts by the amateurs' — the nearest expression of democracy in everyday life.

Whether or not this ultimate responsibility works for the good of the school's pupils is entirely dependent upon one thing: The understanding that professional educationists and lay people have of the distinctive purpose of the governing body. This purpose is to bring together the experience, skills and knowledge of the professional staff, with what the lay governors — and only lay governors — can bring: a unique understanding of the local community and of the expectations and aspirations it has for its children.

What's New about Schools?

A successful school of the early twenty-first century may superficially resemble a successful school of the 1970s. But beneath the surface, there will be a whole new range of factors operating. The most significant of these — and the one that most clearly demonstrates both the complex range of accountabilities the school has, and its more sophisticated ownership — will be the explicit statements of what the school is for, what it does for its students, and what it expects of, or even guarantees for, their experiences, knowledge and skills.

Why Are Targets Important?

Such statements will, in the broadest sense, be targets. As we shall see, they might more usefully be called *promises* or *guarantees*, or even — a term more familiar in the commercial world — *quality standards*. The word *targets* is used throughout this book, because it is used by the government. No school need, legally, do more than set the two or three targets that the DfEE requires, depending on its age-range. Schools dealing with only Key Stages 1 or 3 of the National Curriculum need set no targets at all (at the time of writing). This book is about the range of targets which schools may choose to set. It suggests that governing bodies can adopt target-setting as a strategy to enable them to reinforce their ownership of the school. It sees target-setting as a 'Trojan horse', which governing bodies can use to boost their growing confidence in their own right to set the schools' agenda — sometimes in line with government demands; sometimes, perhaps, in conflict with them. It includes reference to the mandatory targets which the government demands. But it takes such limited target-setting as merely a starting point for a route which will open schools up to a detailed exploration of what they do for our children, of 'what is and what might be' in education.

It will guide governing bodies — and all those parties they recruit to assist them — to an understanding of the different types of targets, and the areas of school activity to which targets can usefully apply. It assumes that governing bodies will wish to recruit a range of parties to help them in the process — the local education authority, who have a statutory role; the staff, both teaching and non-teaching; the parents; the wider school community; and, of course, the pupils themselves.

The wider ownership of schools demands the wider ownership of targets. The setting of school targets, already embarked upon in many local education authorities as a closed, exclusively professional concern, is a debate which can change the way schools operate, provided that all the stakeholders in education play their part. This book is intended to help governing bodies start that debate.

Part I

Measuring Schools

Chapter 1

Who Is Responsible for School Performance?

The governing body is responsible for determining the aims and overall conduct of the school. This includes deciding, with the headteacher, how the
school should develop in order to maintain and improve its standards of
education. (DfEE, 1996b)

Why should governors concern themselves with policy-making? The LEA writes
all our policies . . . The LEA provides the agendas for our governing body meetings and a clerk to assist us. I don't think governors are there to make decisions.
. . . (A secondary school governor, quoted in Walters and Richardson, 1997)

Standards and Frameworks

The governing body is the ultimate authority in a school. It carries the ultimate
responsibility for school performance. It has to answer to the community, and
to the local authority, and to the Secretary of State for Education and Employment. The government's legislation of 1998 (The School Standards and Framework Act) confirmed the place of governors at the heart of the school
improvement movement.

Accountability and the ownership of schools were central to the changes
brought about by the 1998 Education Act:

1 Schools were to be renamed. This was not merely cosmetic. Some of
the motivation here was to find a place within local authority influence
for the former grant-maintained schools. They were not to be brought
back fully into the local education authority (LEA) fold, but would take
their place alongside voluntary-aided schools — self-managed, but
subject to certain LEA influences. At the same time, LEA 'county' schools
were to be called community schools. This would subvert the existing
community schools, designated to demonstrate their role in lifelong
education and the access they offered to the wider community. But
the new name establishes where the *ownership* of schools lies. While
accountability has been part of the rhetoric in education for many
years, and particularly so under the Conservative governments of 1979
to 1997, no mechanisms had been built into the system. 'Each school

should take responsibility for achieving high standards, and should account for its performance to parents and the local community against the standards set by the National Curriculum' (DfEE, 1996a). But apart from the annual duty of the governing body to publish results and report to the parents' meeting, there was no guidance on how to do such accounting. Nor is there any now. Nor, again, is there any formal requirement for schools to account for their performance against *their own standards*. But the renaming of county schools as community schools does remind us of who pays for — and perhaps who rightfully owns — schools.

2   The government already had powers to require LEAs and schools to set targets for improving pupil performance. But the new Act required governing bodies to conduct the school 'with a view to promoting high standards of educational achievement at the school' (DfEE, 1997a). The governing body could also agree that the school could participate in an 'education action zone' — a mechanism for bringing groups of schools and the local community (including Training and Education Councils and local businesses) together to develop action plans, seeking extra funding, tailoring the use of the National Curriculum and operating outside national pay and conditions arrangements for teachers.

3   Local authorities now have powers to intervene in the management of schools where they believe that standards are low, or there is mismanagement. In the past, under the 1996 consolidated act, this amounted to a right to claim that a governing body was acting unreasonably. Now, the LEA can issue a warning notice to governors, can appoint additional governors and, if things are not getting better, suspend the governing body's right to a delegated budget. It can formally object to — though not overrule — the governing body's choice of headteacher. The LEA also has a duty to report to the governors if it is concerned about the performance of the headteacher, and the governing body has to tell the LEA what it means to do about it.

4   The Secretary of State can direct the LEA to intervene where it is failing to give appropriate support to a school, and can direct the governing body to assist the LEA. There are also powers over clerking arrangements, procedures for the election and appointment of governors, and the power to authorize expenses allowances to governors.

5   The governing body will have to adopt a home–school agreement (not a contract — the word was changed so that it did not have the overtones of a legally enforceable agreement), stating the school's aims and values, what the school undertakes to do for the pupils, what parents are expected to do in return (following consultation), and outlining the school's behaviour policy.

6   The governing body is expected to lay down the principles which the head must take into account in preparing the school's behaviour code.

7   The new Standards Fund, replacing Grants for Education Support and Training (GEST) reinstates the ring-fencing of money for governor training (as 6 per cent of the total money provided for training).

Who Does What?

The Role of the Government

The government has taken upon itself the right to set the standards expected from LEAs, schools and school pupils. It takes LEAs to task when they fail to meet these expectations. It determines the broad content of learning through the National Curriculum, the methods of assessment, and it sets the tests. It provides input and outcome targets for schools, and lays its expectations on pupils and their parents (see chapter 2). It has taken on a far more proactive role in school improvement than ever before, with the setting up of education action zones, and intervention in local authorities. It says what it expects to see done on issues such as selection in secondary education, the grouping of pupils in schools, the nature of agreements between parents and schools, and even on the amount of homework expected of 4-year-olds.

Its rhetoric is focused on higher standards — 'everyone concerned with education is committed to doing better' (DfEE, 1997a) — and its understanding of what constitutes 'better' is revealed by its priorities — higher standards of literacy, numeracy, science and information and communication technology. These, linked to national targets for achievement at the four key stages and beyond, are expected to be achieved, even, as some claim, if it is at the expense of the arts, the humanities and, possibly, social, spiritual, moral and cultural education.

The Role of the Inspectorate

Her Majesty's Inspectorate of Schools in England, working through the Office for Standards in Education, similarly, has taken on a far higher profile role. Its primary task is to assist improvement by evaluating schools against criteria laid down by the government. It has also moved into the evaluation of individual teachers, though on very questionable grounds (one school staff decided to burn their assessments without looking at them), and it has made judgments about the effectiveness of governing bodies. It has advised schools generally (not individually) on its views of best practice, based on the data it has collected in the course of inspection. It has therefore assumed — although its qualifications for doing so are suspect — a research and dissemination function.

9

Most controversially, it publishes not only its considered judgment on individual schools, but it finds more and more ways of praising and blaming them. The firmly held opinions of the Chief Inspector at the time of writing reflect a culture which is at odds with the traditional liberal views of the education establishment. LEAs have probably considered the *process* that children experience in schools as at least as significant as the levels of tested competencies that they achieve. They have tended to regard the support of weak schools as more important than the public damnation of them. However, as Ofsted and DfEE pressure mounted, this culture changed perceptibly.

The Role of the LEA

What we have in law is a system of schooling where the governing body is demonstrably in charge, but where checks and balances can be brought into play by the local authority. At the top of the tree is the Secretary of State, who can be brought in, or can step in, when the local structures are not doing their job. Power is much more evenly distributed here than in the past. Formerly the LEA had few powers — little remained after the 1988 Education Reform Act of the Long Knives. Now it has rights and duties to support and intervene, although these are still much more restricted than many local politicians and officers would like.

Table 1.1   LEA powers and duties 1986–98

Before 1986, LEAs could	After 1988, LEAs could	Now LEAs can
Provide	Secure provision	Provide and secure provision
Authorize	Promote	Advise
Direct	Guard a collective vision	Intervene
Inspect	Guarantee (service quality)	Require
Decide	Inform	Support and challenge

The reinvention of local government implies the need for a reassessment of the role of governing bodies. LEAs have rightfully regained much of the power to plan overall educational provision for their area. They also have the duty to make sure that schools are doing their job of raising standards. This they will do in partnership with the school — *provided they agree on the vision of what constitutes raised standards*. The temptation may be to accept the simplistic view preferred by the government — that standards are interpreted as the achievement of acceptable percentages of pupils at the ages of 7, 11, 14 and 16, principally in English, maths and science.

The Role of the Governing Body

Governing bodies, with their unique understanding of the expectations and aspirations of the community they represent, will want to broaden this interpretation. They will want to establish standards across a much wider curriculum;

one that includes social, moral, spiritual and cultural development; that places the taught curriculum in its local context; that sends pupils into the world with the potential to develop into fully-rounded adults.

The governing body which treats with, and works with, its local authority must have a clear sense of what it wants the school to achieve. It will lay down its aims and objectives for the school, and plan all its policies and procedures. It will ensure that the school implements these, and it will monitor pupil progress. And it will evaluate the school's achievements. In all of these activities, it will call in the LEA to help when it needs to.

But the current evidence is that few governing bodies are so assertive. They may be undermined by the professionals within their own school, or by the LEA itself. It is certain that many LEAs have never come to terms with their diminished role in school management. It is equally certain that some LEAs, particularly perhaps some of the new unitary authorities, have viewed the advent of the new government as a signal that they again have a free hand in school management. It is, however, equally certain that the new headteachers — whether they are newly-appointed or 'reborn' — are unlikely to want to lose their authority, an authority which is all the greater than the 'power' they once held, because now it is conferred upon them through the democratic legitimacy of the governing body.

But how do governing bodies, predominantly made up of lay people, monitor and evaluate their schools? They have, of course, as much right and as much responsibility to do it as the professionals, although they come at it from a different angle. There are three levels of judgments which can be made about any service. Table 1.2 shows these judgments when applied to the service provided by a car garage.

Table 1.2   Questions of performance: Judgments of a car garage service

The questions a customer asks — one who knows nothing about cars except driving them	The questions a non-executive director asks — the board having ultimate authority for the business	The questions a managing director asks
Is the service effective? I.e. does my car keep going until the next service?	Do we provide a quality service? Is business growing?	Do I know and do my job?
Is the service reasonably priced?	Is business efficient? Do we offer value for money?	Are we maintaining good budget control?
Is the service comprehensive? (Do I need to open the bonnet between services?)	What complaints do we get?	Do the staff know and do their jobs?
Is the service reliable and pleasant — are people efficient, good to deal with, polite, friendly?	Are we looking after our staff through proper employment procedures? Do we recruit and retain effectively?	Are we keeping staff up-to-date with new developments, and training them effectively?

There is an analogy here with the school governing body — although the process of judging a school is a whole lot more complex (and more likely to affect lives) than a garage. The customer — or parent — will mainly judge by observation. As an ordinary driver, I certainly do not want to look under the car bonnet and understand how it works, any more than the average parent wants to know the detail of how teaching and learning happen. What customers — and parents — need to know is results. Nowadays, parents have a wealth of statistical evidence to use to compare schools. But, despite the best efforts of the Conservative government, they do not all choose schools purely on test results — where they have any choice at all, that is. They consider convenience, of course, but also the way a school presents itself — principally, on the way staff talk to them. Mainly, they seem to make judgments about schools on the basis of how happy their child is, and what (s)he seems to be learning.

The non-executive garage director, and the school governor, having time and interest and commitment beyond the daily customer, as well as a moral and legal responsibility, will bring into play a range of more sophisticated judgments. But these are still essentially *lay* judgments, and require no specialist technical knowledge. They are, however, much enhanced by an understanding of the strategic role of governing body/board of directors. They will involve:

- receiving structured evidence;
- determining future direction: observing in a structured way and planning;
- ensuring action is taken: monitoring;
- receiving evidence of results: evaluating, across a wide range of indicators;
- ensuring that business is conducted ethically, i.e. in line with our organizational values.

The way that governing bodies do these jobs will be looked at in more detail throughout this book.

The Role of the Staff

With all their skills, experience and knowledge, the staff of the school have to implement all the policies thought up by the Secretary of State, the local authority and the governing body. At each level, such policies and procedures will be interpreted (and reinterpreted) by those who are closer to the school. New policies and procedures will be initiated by those at each level — although LEAs may only be able to recommend, not require, their adoption. Both interpretation and initiation should involve those who will be implementing. *This means that the relationship between governors and staff is critical.*

Agenda JOAN SALLIS answers your questions (*TES*, 20 March 1998)

Q Over the years the headteacher has moved a long way towards a sharing relationship with governors at our comprehensive.

But we work in a compartment sealed off from the rest of the school. The bulk of the teachers seem to know nothing about why schools have governors or what we do and I would say their attitude ranges from indifference to slightly mocking hostility.

Middle management is little better.

Surely they ought to be thinking about the people who, in the end, decide their staffing and department budgets and whom they will wish to influence if their department is ever in trouble, even if they don't think about being senior managers themselves one day?

Even the deputy heads have little direct involvement. Am I right to worry about this?

Indifference and slightly mocking hostility may not be the most helpful basis for a relationship between employer and employee. All planning and all target-setting, therefore, should involve staff beyond the membership of the governing body.

The role of the staff in relation to school governance is to:

- provide governors with accurate and timely information on the implementation and evaluation of policies and procedures;
- inform governors of other issues which may need consideration as they arise;
- advise on the law;
- advise on national and local policy;
- advise on good practice elsewhere;
- participate in policy formulation, including carrying out or facilitating consultation.

This 'job description' for teachers and other staff in their relationship to school policy-making clarifies the nature of the partnership. The governing body brings both community knowledge and professional expertise to the task, but it cannot be effective without calling on *all* the expertise it has at its disposal. Nor will it take the 'faceworkers' with it, if it does not consult and listen. Staff and governors need each other, as surely as they need the pupils and the parents, if the school is to continuously improve.

The sooner teachers are seen as knowledge workers, professional educators and leaders, the sooner schools will improve. (Stoll and Fink, 1996, p. 6)

The Role of the Parents

Parents are given a stronger role in the 1998 Act. There are more of them on governing bodies, and they have a say on LEA education committees. Every school has to have a written home–school agreement, drawn up in consultation with parents: 'This will explain the respective responsibilities of the school and parents, and what the school expects of its pupils. Parents will be asked to endorse the agreement after their child's entry to the school' (DfEE, 1997a).

Simultaneously, parents are being reminded of their legal obligations on pupils' attendance; and the expectations the school has on discipline and homework.

However, for the DfEE, parents are only recipients in school target-setting: 'There is no expectation or requirement that parents will become involved in individual or school target-setting' (DfEE, 1997c). Good schools already involve parents in individual target-setting, and many will consult their parent body on collective targets.

Similarly, while there is an expectation that home–school agreements will be contracts (albeit unenforceable in law) between notionally equal partners, there has been less emphasis on what schools will be expected to commit themselves to. In chapter 3, we will be looking at what parents might reasonably expect of schools in terms of guarantees. Target-setting for pupil achievement is also about target-setting for school achievement. This suggests that schools should be able to articulate to parents a set of basic commitments. No public service should do less.

The Question to Address

The roles of all the stakeholders in schools have altered, in some cases dramatically, since the Education Acts of the early 1980s. The changes in the expectations of the governing body are perhaps the most far-reaching of all. This may have been about confirming the *ownership* of the school by the community rather than by the educational establishment, or it may have been an attempt to give a clearer and more public definition of the *accountability* of schools. Whatever the motive, governing bodies have found themselves at the centre of school improvement initiatives. This has concentrated minds wonderfully. Given that the governing body has a distinctive role to play in raising standards, how can governors make a difference to the quality of education offered? What is a realistic way to set targets that raises morale and achievement among staff and students? What action can a governing body take to improve a school?

Chapter 2

What Do We Mean by Targets?

What Is the First Step in Target-setting?

What is education about? Who are schools for?

The government has provided its own definition in the form of the national curriculum, and all the other requirements it lays on schools. Local authorities have limited powers and duties to determine whether or not a school is effective — in their own terms. They can intervene when they think it isn't. But the priorities of individual schools are still the responsibility of the people on the ground. What those priorities should be, and how they are reflected in practice, is still up to the governing body.

Whether education is primarily developmental or functional — whether it is about developing the individual or providing material to meet society's needs — has been the subject of debate in this country for as long as schools have been around. In the twentieth century, this debate has become public property.

In 1911, for example, former HMI Edmond Holmes wrote:

> My aim in writing this book is to show that the *externalism* of the West, the prevalent tendency to pay undue regard to outward and visible 'results' and to neglect what is inward and vital, is the source of most of the defects that vitiate education in this country . . .
>
> The function of education is to foster growth. The end which the teacher should set before himself is the development of the latent powers of his pupils, the unfolding of their latent life. If growth is to be fostered, two things must be liberally provided — nourishment and exercise . . . The process of growing must be done by the growing organism, by the child. (p. 3)

This polarization of views has inevitably reflected the debate about ownership of the education system:

> The very idea of elementary education sprang from pity for poor folk who could *not* organize, could *not* pay, could *not* realize what was good for their children. It is not surprising, therefore, that the organizers of schooling from the first compulsory Act of 1870 to the last of 1918 treated 'the parent' as a prospective enemy, to be coerced by threat of summons and penalty. (Findlay, 1923, p. 103)

Put simply, if schools are provided by the state to train young people to meet the needs of the state (as 'the state' sees those needs), then the content of education can be determined by the state — through Parliament, through the Civil Service, through local government, and through the education establishment. This then begs the question, 'Who comprises — or who owns — the state?'

But if 'education is development from within and . . . based upon natural endowments' (Dewey, 1938, p. 32), then at least a share of the ownership of schools belongs to the people.

So the debate about quality, about standards, about the statement, 'everyone concerned with education is committed to doing better' (DfEE, 1997a) avoids the critical question: 'Better at what?'

This has to be answered at school level. An equivocal reply was given by Prime Minister James Callaghan in his seminal 'Ruskin College' speech, an occasion often seen as the springboard from which all subsequent government decision-making on education has developed:

> The goals of our education, from nursery school through to adult education, are clear enough. *They are to equip children to the best of their ability for a lively, constructive place in society and also to fit them to do a job of work.* Not one or the other, but both. (quoted in Barber, 1996)

This response may confront the question of the national context of education. But it does little or nothing to help individual schools develop policies on the curriculum — on teaching styles, on grouping of children, on relationships between home and school. The tensions articulated by Holmes in 1911 were revived — eventually to become a *cause célèbre* in the 1970s:

> The deschooling of society implies a recognition of the two-faced nature of learning. An insistence on skill–drill alone could be a disaster; equal emphasis must be placed on other kinds of learning. But if schools are the wrong places for learning a skill, they are even worse places for getting an education. School does both tasks badly, partly because it does not distinguish between them. School is inefficient in skill instruction especially because it is curricular. In most schools a programme which is meant to improve one skill is chained always to another irrelevant task. History is tied to advancement in maths, and class attendance to the right to use the playground. Schools are even less efficient in the arrangement of the circumstances which encourage the open-ended, exploratory use of acquired skills, for which I will reserve the term 'liberal education'. The main reason for this is that school is obligatory and becomes schooling for schooling's sake: an enforced stay in the company of teachers, which pays off in the doubtful privilege of more such company. Just as skill instruction must be freed from curricular restraints, so must liberal education be dissociated from obligatory attendance. (Illich, 1971, p. 24)

The centrality of testing, judgment by league tables, the laying down of homework requirements, all promote a narrow view of achievement. The emphasis of all recent governments on such performance measures inevitably affects what schools do and how they do it. HMI Holmes wrote from the experience of inspecting schools in an age of rampant functionalism. Payment by results imposed a rigid testing and coaching regime which was almost a caricature of a centrally-imposed system. During the first three-quarters of the twentieth century, teachers complained of the straitjacketing of the curriculum by 11-plus testing, and by the powerful, university-dominated examination boards. After 1965, the Certificate of Secondary Education allowed — for those with some imagination — a brief flowering of a school-centred examination for some pupils. But 100 years on from the system that Holmes reviled, what do we have?

> I am 11 years old and am doing my SATs test from May 11–15. I am writing to you to give a public complaint that already we have studied for six weeks roughly. We have gone through things that we have done at least three times (eg sound, light and electricity). I think we should be learning new things instead like history, which is just as important as maths but not in the test. It does not do anything to our career, it only tests the teachers and, if you get good marks, makes the school look good. So why do we have to be put through all this pressure? (Letter to the Guardian from Rosie Sherwood of London, 17 March 1998)

Only governing bodies are in a position to resist this culture.

What Are the Key Issues that Governing Bodies Discuss?

This conflict, which is at the heart of the educational debate, is often reflected in governing bodies by a series of oppositions. Sometimes the debate appears on the margins of the agenda, rearing its head time and time again, to waste precious time and to exasperate the many. It clearly needs to be dealt with, not in 'business', but in an open sharing of values and priorities. Table 2.1 shows some of the issues that governing bodies might discuss that reflect this debate.

Table 2.1   The polarities of school debates

Selection	v	comprehensive schooling
Uniform	v	non-uniform
'Traditional' teaching styles	v	'modern' teaching styles
Open-plan classrooms	v	desks in rows
Integration/inclusiveness	v	segregation
Homework	v	no homework
'Real books'	v	phonics
Horizontal grouping	v	vertical grouping
Education ethic	v	business ethic
Security	v	open access
Needs-led budget	v	formula budget

Although governors rarely hold such polarized views as presented here, these and similar issues lie at the heart of the strategic decisions that governing bodies make. How many have debated them as principles to be affirmed or denied? Or do we rather deal with individual cases as they arise, without a clear and openly articulated ethical standpoint?

> *The first task in target-setting is for the governing body — taking into account the views of the largest possible number of stakeholders — to determine the school's stance on the fundamental issues. The values of the school come first. Targets make sense only in the context of the values.*

What are these key values?

At the heart of the debate — not just in England and Wales — are quality and equality:

> The reforms proposed in most countries have been made in the name of quality and efficiency. They provide the rhetoric of equity but fail to accommodate the changing nature of society. Indeed many changes tend to be ways for the 'haves' to escape from the 'have nots'. Grant-maintained schools in Britain which have become selective in their intake, American charter schools which choose their clientele, and various choice and voucher initiatives are popular political responses which gain favour with the affluent but ignore the impact of postmodernity on the least empowered elements of society. (Stoll and Fink, 1996, p. 7)

The quality/equality debate which has been at the heart of British politics over two decades is critical to the values of each individual school: will wealth, quality of health care, transport, education trickle down to raise quality for all in a free market? Or is positive action necessary to ensure that the poor, the sick, the old, the disadvantaged, those whom education excludes, receive a share of the rewards of the affluent society?

The school's stance on this issue is fundamental to the process of target-setting. This will become obvious as we discuss the types of targets which schools may set, the areas in which they set them, the ways in which targets are negotiated and communicated. It is difficult to conceive of a governing body going about target-setting in the curriculum, to take just one area, without having sorted out its collective attitude to what Stoll and Fink call the 'quality–equity paradox'. It permeates every debate in the school, and is at the heart of the polarized positions listed in table 2.1.

The obvious time and place for this debate is during the review of the aims of the curriculum. Drawing these up is a statutory responsibility of the whole governing body. Monitoring and reviewing them is the core part of school development planning. The form the debate takes may vary. In one secondary school, one staff in-service training day each year is devoted to a day for staff and governors (sometimes involving parents, the wider community and pupils), to discuss an all-embracing issue. In recent years, topics have

Table 2.2   Factors for effective schools

1	**Professional leadership**	Firm and purposeful A participative approach The leading professional
2	**Shared vision and goals**	Unity of purpose Consistency of practice Collegiality and collaboration
3	**A learning environment**	An orderly atmosphere An attractive working environment
4	**Concentration on teaching and learning**	Maximization of learning time Academic emphasis Focus on achievement
5	**High expectations**	High expectations all round Communicating expectations Providing intellectual challenge
6	**Positive reinforcement**	Clear and fair discipline Feedback
7	**Monitoring progress**	Monitoring pupil performance Evaluating school performance
8	**Pupil rights and responsibilities**	High pupil self-esteem Positions of responsibility Control of work
9	**Purposeful teaching**	Efficient organization Clarity of purpose Structured lessons Adaptive practice
10	**A learning organization**	School-based staff development
11	**Home–school partnership**	Parental involvement

(Sammons et al, 1995)

included: Reviewing the school development plan; the school behaviour policy; 'sharing our values'; drawing up a person specification for a new headteacher. All of these issues require participants to identify what they believe the purpose of schooling to be — but to do so in a pragmatic way, founding theory in day-to-day practice.

We are familiar with lists of elements of school effectiveness. These are frequently circulated amongst the academic establishment. One is reproduced in table 2.2.

Each school reflects its own values in the way that it prioritizes these factors.

While such lists are commonplace in the educational establishment, they are more rarely seen in schools. They raise the kind of questions that seem only to become significant when, for example, a new headteacher is being appointed. Is an emphasis on pupil rights a higher priority than creating a learning environment? Does the need for an effective home–school partnership sometimes override the need for consistency of practice? These are useful discussion points for governing bodies. They raise practical and ethical issues which have a profound impact on the way an individual school operates — its policies and procedures, its relationships and its desired outcomes.

Stoll and Fink (1996, pp. 32–5) list factors which predict ineffectiveness in schools: Lack of vision; unfocused leadership; dysfunctional staff relationships; ineffective classroom practices. It is clear that these elements are within the remit of the governing body *and of no other agency.*

This is not to say that a school with these characteristics always does bad work. As Rossini said of Wagner's music, it may have good moments, but bad quarters of an hour. But, as Schein (1985) has argued: possibly the 'only thing of real importance that leaders do is to create and manage culture' (p. 2). So, to balance the emphasis on academic results laid down by the school improve-ment movement, Stoll and Fink (1996) remind us of 'the one ingredient that underlies all the concepts we have described, one which will make or break the change process: caring. It not only provides the moral purpose for change, . . . it also adds the ethic which invites pupils, teachers, principals, parents and all those interested in educational change to join, contribute and persevere on the change journey' (p. 192).

What Are Governors For, Anyway?

We would not expect to spend time on innovations in education that did not, *overall*, improve the quality of schooling. However, we should not lose sight of the possibility that school governance — that is, local ownership of schools — may not be primarily a matter of school effectiveness in the short term. It may be more of an issue of social inclusion. It is, therefore, a political matter. Of course, school effectiveness *is* a political issue. Despite the apparent con-sensus across the major political parties, 'effective at what?' is the question begged by much of the school improvement movement. Do we accept that school effectiveness is about being effective at getting higher proportions of children past the highest possible level at each key stage? Is there national consensus that the National Curriculum has got it right (in every one of its manifestations)? Is there not an issue — still — about what schools are for?

> Not only are schools in the business of developing good learners, they are in the business of developing good people . . . (a) metaphor is the school as a caring family. In contrast to dysfunctional families and ineffective schools, consider how truly functional and caring families and improving schools work. They have high expectations for all their members; they build on and recog-nize individual strengths while providing mutual support; they compensate and help individual weaknesses; and they behave in ways based on mutual trust, respect, optimism and intentionality. Learning communities are caring families. (ibid)

Where there does seem to be consensus is that schools and families should work together to help children grow *and* learn. And there is concern about the extent to which parents — especially those who feel socially excluded — support what schools are doing. Hence the cascade of legislation and exhortation about home–school agreements, about homework, about after-school clubs and school exclusion — and about behaviour in schools and the behaviour and achievement of boys.

Everyone agrees that schools work best with the consent and the active support and involvement of parents and the wider community. In fact, most of us would say that schools cannot work at all without them. School governance is a way of asserting parental and community ownership of a professional process.

So Where Might Targets Fit In?

The culture of the school will be formulated and expressed in the way that schools go about target-setting, and in the nature of the targets they set. A governing body which starts out on the target-setting journey needs the following agenda:

Decide what your school is for
Agree what you want pupils to do
Agree what you want pupils to be able to do
Find — and benchmark against — other schools that have similar values
Decide how your school will achieve your vision.

Chapter 3

Target-setting: What Is and What Might Be

New Controllers — New Controls

The 1997 General Election was a landslide for Labour. The new regime at the Department for Education and Employment decided on a combination of carrot and stick (DfEE, 1997a) to push forward its school improvement regime. The pressure would involve:

- setting challenging national and local targets;
- having 'tough' negotiations with local authorities on benchmarking categories, on the mandatory targets for schools, and on the optional targets for schools.

The support would comprise:

- quality information on national and local patterns, from the Qualifications and Curriculum Authority (QCA) and Ofsted;
- support for school management and leadership;
- requirements for local authorities to produce an Education Development Plan.

The counting and the planning that were to happen would make the communist states of the earlier part of the century look as if they were making things up as they went along. Everything that teachers did with children was to be legislated or regulated; every measurable outcome would be counted; every policy would be directed.

Schools would be required to:

(i)   set a single target for each of the three core subjects at the end of each Key Stage. At KS1, from the tests in reading, writing and mathematics: 'it seems sensible to express school targets as the proportion of pupils, subject by subject, reaching level 2 or above'; at KS2, after the tests in English, mathematics and science: 'school target-setting should use achievements at Level 4 in all subjects'; at KS3 (following tests in English, mathematics and science): 'it seems sensible to express school targets as the proportion of pupils, subject by subject, reaching Level 5 or above' (DfEE, 1997a). These targets were revised later (see p. 36);

(ii)   have additional optional targets;

(iii)   choose the comparator category/categories (probably prior attainment and the proportion eligible for free school meals).

The Logic of Target-setting

Target-setting is supposed to concentrate the minds of the school — mainly the minds of the staff — on *measurable achievement*. As it is presented by the government, it says:

This is what is important —
What is important can be measured —
What is measured can be achieved —
What is achieved can be shown to have been achieved.

Target-setting is therefore absolutely dependent on information accurately gathered and communicated.

We have many kinds of information nowadays about schools. Most of this has grown out of inspection, and out of the tests associated with the National Curriculum. This is the information we have, *therefore* these are the factors that will be used to make judgments about schools. Schools will therefore be able to say: 'We improve, therefore we are.' Deciding what is important is, however, as we have seen, another matter. Some American management writers claim that 'If you can't measure it, you can't manage it'. Whether or not you can value it — even if you can't measure it — is another matter.

Sadly, even the measurements we have of schools are either suspect in the way they are collected, or limited in their understanding of what schools are for. This is not to suggest that we should not have as much information as possible. What is suggested is that much of the information we have — collected and delivered by the DfEE and Ofsted — is inaccurate and sometimes dangerously misleading.

What's the Matter with School Inspection?

(i)   Inspection of schools under the current system is too fleeting and its methodology too suspect to gather a true picture of how the school is performing. Is school inspection an attempt at quality assurance? That is, is it 'the determination of standards, appropriate methods and quality requirements by an expert body, accompanied by a process of inspection or evaluation that examines the extent to which practices meet these

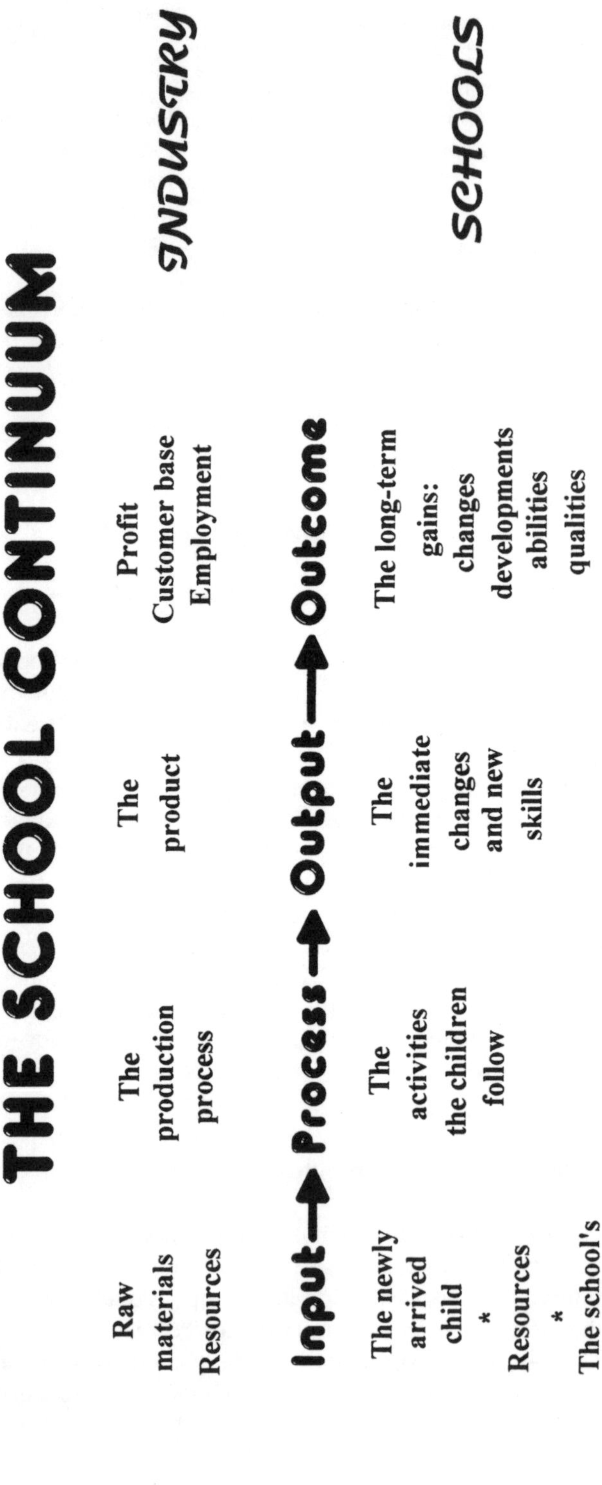

Figure 3.1 The school continuum

THE SCHOOL CONTINUUM

INDUSTRY

Input →	Process →	Output →	Outcome
Raw materials Resources	The production process	The product	Profit Customer base Employment

SCHOOLS

Input →	Process →	Output →	Outcome
The newly arrived child * Resources * The school's priorities	The activities the children follow	The immediate changes and new skills	The long-term gains: changes developments abilities qualities

standards' (Murgatroyd and Morgan, 1993, p. 45)? Or is it quality control ('a process which is directed at checking and inspecting a process after it has been completed and ensuring that it is acceptable') (Lawrie, 1992, p. 49)? Actually, Ofsted tries to do *both* these things, in a visit of between three and five days every four to six years. The decision to inspect less frequently *only* those schools which appear to have outputs which are average or higher than expected — regardless of input — suggests that Ofsted is leaning towards quality control rather than quality assurance. But quality control is an activity that institutions conduct for themselves, because it has to be happening all the time. Quality assurance looks at systems; quality control at outcomes. If Ofsted were truly interested in quality assurance, they would spend the little time they have ensuring that effective systems were in place, and were being implemented. Spending time in classrooms would not be their job. And rightly so. We do not need to be statisticians to know that the judgments of teachers' lessons are based on too small a sample, and are too unreliable (that is, not sufficiently reproducible) to be of any real value. We know that different inspectors make different assessments of the same lesson and of the same teacher; that teachers are observed in very different circumstances; that different inspection teams come up with different judgments about schools (see, for example, Fitz-Gibbon, 1996). An unreliable inspection system — one that does not have the confidence of the parents or of the teachers — may be worse than no inspection system at all. Its very unreliability makes good schools sceptical and gives poor schools an excuse to dismiss criticism.

(ii)   The methods adopted by Ofsted are inappropriate. If you want to see how a school is really performing, you need to collect and then *analyse* results, so that you can see the outcomes set against the inputs, that is, the material the school has to work with in order to produce results in the way the DfEE measures them. You then need to 'parachute' into schools without warning, so you can see how teachers behave on an ordinary day, when they didn't think anyone outside was looking. Some judgments of what schools are like can then be made on the evidence of *cooked* results (see figure 3.1) and *raw* behaviour. Cooked results provide us with an overview of what the school has achieved for its children in the light of the child *and* of the school. While schools still have the freedom to do things other than prepare children for National Curriculum tests, it is important that they are judged by their performance in these things. The current system of inspection, however, does neither of these things. It does not sufficiently allow for the school's inputs. Nor does it allow for the preparation that takes place, given six months or more warning. Contrariwise, it focuses only on *raw results* and on *cooked behaviour.* Consequently, there has been little correlation between Ofsted judgments and the use of value added data. Such data was available to Ofsted from 1996, but it has not been used, in case it gave 'under-performing schools' an excuse. However, we know from research undertaken by the University of Durham that 59 out of 83 'failing' secondary schools are in areas with poverty levels of at least twice the national average. So either schools in disadvantaged areas are more than twice as bad as other schools, or Ofsted is failing to take disadvantage properly into account in making its judgments. We also know (*TES*, 22 May 1998) that 18 per cent of the primary schools that were failed between the summer of 1997 and spring 1998 were 'actually making good progress in English and maths when their results are analysed using the benchmark methods devised by the Qualifications and Curriculum Authority; (Pyke, 1998, p. 3).

(iii)   Ofsted aims are confused. It has been intended to do two things — to inspect schools individually, in order to determine, and to publish, how they are performing according to its own criteria. At the same time, it has contributed to a database which holds information about every school in the country. It has then drawn conclusions from this information, and published them. It has acted simultaneously as inspector and researcher — two roles which might be thought to be irreconcilable. But, as we have seen, the data collected has been unadjusted. It has led to some questionable conclusions — that class size is not a factor in children's learning; that formal classroom organization is more effective than informal grouping. When Her Majesty's Chief Inspector (HMCI) reports his findings formally to Parliament, he makes a range of such judgments. On the one hand, he acknowledges that teachers have 'to deal with the tragic consequences of family breakdown, long-term unemployment, and poor housing'. In the same document, he suggests that it is 'ever more difficult for less successful schools to blame failure on factors beyond the school's control' (Ofsted, 1998a). HMCI reports make sweeping statements which would seem to support progress made by the legislators: 'Four years ago, the idea that any teacher might be incompetent was dismissed as a ludicrous right-wing plot' (ibid). They produce figures which appear to be evidence — until we remember how they have been collected, in the course of a three–five day visit: 'Homework makes a positive contribution in one-third of secondary schools; in one-sixth it is ineffective.' And these judgments lead to government policy and legislation. Since it would seem that in the majority of secondary schools, homework makes no positive contribution, it might make sense to suggest that it should be done away with. Instead, government policy determines that all secondary schools will set homework every night. Thus a spurious authority is accorded to statements dismissing tried and tested teaching techniques. Inspectors have not been trained as researchers. As has been pointed out, the first Director of Ofsted was a part-time professor of theology; the second was an English teacher. It is not likely that either could boast a track record of statistical analysis. The confusion over judging schools against national norms and expectations was therefore predictable. When judgments are published, schools 'named and shamed', and when schools may be labelled as 'failures', we might have expected some rigour in setting boundaries. However, in its early years, Ofsted did not apply such standards to itself:

'Ofsted does not define the terms raised in this question', wrote the HMCI in reply to a parliamentary question from Dale Campbell-Savours MP (reported in the *TES*, March/April 1998). 'Terms such as "in line with national expectations" are those chosen by inspectors to give their view of standards in a subject. When evaluating and reporting on what pupils achieve, inspectors must report on "how the attainment of pupils at each stage of education compares with national averages in terms of results at key stage tests and assessments or, where these are not available, expectations for the age group concerned". Expectations for the age group concerned are those defined by the National Curriculum.' These are the very expectations that were simultaneously being questioned by the HMCI himself: 'It may well be that the Key Stage 1 test results produce too optimistic a picture of pupil progress. Take reading. Level 2 is the national expectation for 7-year-olds. Level 2 covers a broad range of attainment and is subdivided into three grades. Four-fifths of pupils reach grade 2C which is the least demanding, about three-fifths reach grade 2B and only about two-fifths reach the most demanding grade 2A. If, as many believe, grade 2C is pitched too low, then the test does not represent a proper stepping-stone to Key Stage 2 and may be depressing teacher and pupil' (ibid, p. 13).

What is actually happening here is that a group of experts has determined what level of reading is appropriate to a particular chronological age. When systematic tests have been applied, it is discovered that 80 per cent of children achieve that level. It might have been useful to celebrate that success for our children and teachers before moving on to raise expectations. Instead, it is 'discovered' that the test is 'pitched too low'. A little earlier, HMCI writes that 'Above all, expectations must be raised as to what is possible'. It is inconsistent to use expectations as both a judgment *and* a target. If it is a target — as it seems to be used here — it is somewhat naive to berate schools for failing to help children reach it when the target is raised as soon as they have. A similar technique was employed by earlier governments, who brought into question the standards of GCSE and Advanced Level examinations when the success rate of pupils rose.

(iv) Judgments of whole schools may have been inappropriate, where the variation between the performance of departments within a school can be greater than the variations between the performances of different schools. To damn an entire school on the basis of one or two departments (or one or two teachers) may be akin to keeping the whole class in detention because someone talked out of turn — but with rather more far-reaching effects.

(v)   Finally, Ofsted outcomes do not necessarily bear any relationship to judgments made on other imperfect but rather more structured grounds. Comparison between maths and English results adjusted for intake, using the benchmarks developed by the QCA, shows that at least 18 per cent of failed primary schools were achieving above expectations (*TES*, 22 May 1998). The evidence that schools in disadvantaged areas are much more likely to fail than others is very strong, even though many of them seem to be doing a pretty good job.

What's the Matter with the Measuring of Schools?

We have a number of ways now of seeing how schools and how children are performing. Unfortunately, these are sometimes confused with each other, when they may be quite different systems. Certainly, measurement systems have different purposes. All the systems provide important information for schools, for LEAs, for the DfEE and for parents. But they also have serious limitations, which governing bodies need to take into account.

Baseline assessment is the first identification of children's learning needs in schools. As far as measurement is concerned, it not only diagnoses what children need to learn, but it places the child at a point on the starting grid so that all subsequent measurements have something to which to be compared. Subsequent judgments can then be made on how the child is doing, and how the school is affecting what the child is doing. Schools can choose their own assessment scheme. Nationally, there were some ninety schemes available in 1998, the year in which baseline assessment became compulsory. Many of these, it has been claimed by Professor Geoff Lindsay, Director of the Special Needs Research Unit at the University of Warwick's School of Education, 'whose technical quality we have no knowledge of. If this is the case, how can we judge effectiveness? How can we compare schools and local authorities? There is no way that a valid comparison can be made.' (British Psychological Society conference, reported in *TES*, March 1998). Once again, the obvious advantages of initial diagnosis are diluted by the methods that are in place.

While some of the schemes in themselves may have been questionable, the methods of administering them also varied. For the process to be used as a valid comparison between children and schools — and for them to be used to compare children for the next 11 years — each reception class teacher in every school in every local authority in the country will be administering the same scheme in the same way. Unfortunately, such teachers, conscientious as they may be — are hardly disinterested examiners. They will certainly not want to overestimate a child's skills, as this is likely to rebound on them in all subsequent tests, especially at the published end of Key Stage 1 tests.

The situation is further confused by the fact that some parents will want their 4 and 5-year-olds to perform better than they might otherwise do. In the spring of 1998, parents were warned by the DfEE not to coach their children towards the assessments. In order to appeal to the ambitious parent, play-groups and nursery schools in some areas offer coaching.

Indispensable as the tests are as diagnostic tools, their usefulness as measures of school intake is limited.

Standardized Assessment Tasks

Using SATs results to evaluate a school's performance is not as simple as reading off positions in a league table. Governors need to take these issues into consideration:

- The tests change every year, so we have to be cautious in using them to compare one year group to another;
- The delivery of the tests is in the hands of the teachers who — as in baseline assessment — are not disinterested in the results. Unlike baseline assessment, however, teachers will have to take some responsibility for the children's results. It will therefore not be in their interest to *under*estimate. We may, perhaps, not be surprized to see some quite startling improvements in children's attainment between entering school and the end of Key Stage 1. This perhaps cynical view was nevertheless confirmed by the QCA's decision in May 1998 to conduct random checks on 2000 of the schools conducting national tests at Key Stages 1, 2 and 3 — just in case some schools were cheating. The QCA claimed that schools might be opening test papers early to give last-minute coaching, putting answers up on the blackboard during the test, and allowing pupils to improve their answers after the test, so as to improve their results. Thirty cases of malpractice had been formally investigated in the previous year, and 10 were proved.
- In the interests of improving scores, there has been some coaching. Some children do mock tests weekly from Christmas until May. Their performance cannot be genuinely compared with those from schools who believe that the testing regime should be as unpressurized as possible.
- SATs only measure a narrow range of skills, basic as those skills may be. They do not tell us much about children's ability to learn, or about their personal and social development.

Once again, like inspection and baseline assessment, SATs are doing two jobs which may be incompatible. First, they are diagnosing, so that teachers can identify the needs of individual children. In which case, there is no need to publish them. Secondly, they are used to evaluate the school and the teachers. In which case, why inspect? Fitz-Gibbon (1996, pp. 74–77) gives a more detailed analysis of the problems with SATs tests. She lists a potential threat to student–teacher relationships, the dangers of negative labelling of children and schools, the unavoidable bias in internal assessment in favour of the results which will serve the teacher best, and the unreasonable workload demanded of teachers.

Measurements of School Intake

If we are governing or managing a school, we will be more interested in how *schools* are doing than in how individual *children* are doing. That is, we need to measure the progress that children make — some of which (we don't know how much) will be due to the school — rather than their attainment. For this reason, we need to know at what level the children come to us, in any area of work. Baseline assessment and end of Key Stage tests (not forgetting the other measures that schools use, such as reading tests) try to answer these questions.

But we also need to know to what extent the children's progress is supported or hampered by other issues — areas over which neither the school nor the child has any control.

Socioeconomic Measures

In the spring of 1998, Ofsted started to provide schools with information which would allow them to compare their starting points rather than their finishing places. The Performance and Assessment Reports (PANDAs) acknowledge that, while 'schools in similar social contexts obtain widely differing outcomes' (Ofsted, 1998b), the socioeconomic status of a school's catchment area does have an undetermined impact on the performance of the children. Of course, there are many things that aren't measured, and many things that aren't measurable. We can assume that increasing efforts will be made to establish what schools can do and what they can't. We don't know why some children attain high levels of educational achievement, while others from identical backgrounds *as far as they can be measured*, don't. The way the measuring system works at present is that the responsibility for all those things which can't be, or aren't, measured, is put down to the school. What we do know about children is their measurable prior attainment — which probably explains some 50 per cent of the variations in children's achievement. We can also measure some socio-economic factors which, according to some research, explains as much as 92 per cent of variations in achievement (see, for example, Stoll and Fink, 1996). Between 14 per cent and 50 per cent of variation remains, which is currently unexplained and unmeasurable — the bits we don't know about, or don't know how to count. This is the bit of progress for which schools take the praise or, more frequently, the blame. Perhaps we should concentrate on finding out about these? Are they about emotional background? Parental support? Genetics? These can be dangerous questions, but they are begged by the PANDA approach.

PANDAs work on the assumption that the socioeconomic data of the surrounding districts — listed as electoral wards — can 'give a broad proxy indication of the prior attainment of schools' pupils overall' (Ofsted, 1998b, p. 3). Figures are drawn from the latest census, and include the proportion of adults with higher education, children in high social class households, children of minority ethnic origin and children in overcrowded households. There are weaknesses in this assumption. The surrounding districts will not send children to the school in an evenly distributed way. No attempt was made in the first set of PANDAs to make an adjustment for the proportion of children coming from each of the wards listed. Schools on the edges of their LEAs, particularly, will not draw equally upon areas of equal distance, while transport facilities and local history will impact on sources of children. Catchment areas are to some extent historical. It is therefore quite possible that a school bordering comparatively affluent areas will draw disproportionately few children from there, and disproportionately larger numbers from disadvantaged areas further away. They become more misleading, of course, as the time lengthens since the last full census.

Nevertheless, collectible figures show that school location does have a significant effect on a school's results. Car ownership and unemployment figures are included in the Townsend Index commonly used for predicting health care provision. If these are added to the data given in PANDAs, we can see that location may account for more than half of the variance between secondary schools in GCSE results (Conduit et al). However, accurate measures of prior attainment — which allow for socioeconomic circumstances — are the most reliable baseline measure for schools.

PANDAs include, and are partly founded on, the Qualifications and Curriculum Authority (QCA) 'benchmarks' for schools. These provide a guide to the range of attainment levels achieved by children adjusted according to the school's intake. School intake is categorized, for primary schools, according to the percentage of pupils for whom English is an additional language, and the percentage of pupils eligible for free school meals. In secondary schools, the benchmarks take into account whether the school is selective, as well as eligibility for free meals. (The data for eligibility for free meals has been collected in a variety of ways throughout the country, and probably varies in reliability.) There is also some concern that the breadth of the bands in which schools have been placed still leaves the least advantaged catchment areas at a disadvantage.

Benchmarking

The QCA usage of the term 'benchmark' is unusual. The dictionary defines a benchmark as 'anything taken or used as a point of reference or comparison, a standard, criterion, etc'. Commonly, benchmarking is a method used in industry to compare processes, and sometimes outputs, not inputs. What industry normally does *not* do is to compare the raw materials it uses with those used by its competitors. If it were to, and found that its raw material was not so good, it would presumably either try to improve its purchasing process, or it would settle for a lower quality — but cheaper — product. What industry and business do is to look for the *best* examples of *practice* they can find in their own and allied services. They then use what they have seen to help them brush up their own ways of doing things. They will look at best health and safety practice, reception practice, marketing, accounting and management methods, as well as direct production techniques. Clearly, doing this, they will consider some input and output measurements — the number of units produced, profitability, degrees of customer satisfaction, and so on. But benchmarking itself focuses on a process. The question it asks is — how could this thing that we do be done better?

Industry benchmarks the best; education benchmarks the rest

Now this would be a very useful practice for our schools. We could see that our maths department, for example, is not producing as good results as our English department; that progress in year 3 is slower than in year 2; that parents aren't involved in our school as much as they are in the school down the road. To do this, we need to be able to locate schools that do it better, so that we can find out how and why. PANDAs are not designed to help with this.

What the QCA is telling us is rather different. It has constructed a national performance rating for the schools which seem to have intakes which are a bit like ours. It is a norm-based system where, once the median performance is set, the same number of schools will outstrip the 'benchmark' as will fail to reach it. It is a system where some schools — it will always be about 25 per cent — must fail.

The guidance for governors on target-setting (DfEE, 1997c) suggests that there are three questions to be asked at the benchmarking stage:

- How well should our school be doing?
- How well do schools like ours perform?
- Are we among the best schools of our type?

The information collected for schools leaves some serious gaps for governors following this model. We are unlikely to be clear about how our school is doing against the criteria used by the QCA and Ofsted. The QCA figures assume what is 'best' by those elements of the school it is able to measure. We need first to define what we — the governing body — think is 'best'. Then we need information about *how* to make things better.

What's the Theory Behind Target-setting?

Are Targets 'A Good Thing'?

In the current blizzard of target-setting, there has been no evidence presented that setting a target actually improves performance. While absence of evidence is not evidence of absence, it is a poor platform from which to launch a national policy. Setting a target for people in their work without first helping them to look at the systems which produce their results is marking some of them for failure for which they may not be 'to blame'. Failing people — teachers, parents and children — for working in systems which are beyond their control is purely destructive.

The first requirement to improve systems is to adopt a quality approach. Measuring and inspection which exclude the people responsible for the systems — the staff and the governing body — are unlikely to improve the system. It is now nearly a century since 'scientific' methods of management were introduced into industry. The key tenet of the most influential proponent of scientific management, Frederick Taylor, was 'developing effective procedures of supervision and uniform standards of production, and from there integrating the human and technical sides of the industrial process' (Bottery, 1992, p. 23). 'In the past', Taylor wrote (Taylor, 1911, p. 7), 'the man has been first; in the future, the system must be first'. In other words, Taylor saw that there was one solution to each problem, whatever the individual circumstances. This solution relied on the manager, not the worker, taking responsibility for the process; on identifying the best worker, and training everyone else so that they could replicate him. This, alongside rigorous monitoring, would produce the ideal, or the close to ideal, process. This philosophy has been preeminent in some parts of the world of education. So there might be one successful method of teaching to be recommended, one amount of homework for all children of a particular age, one target of achievement or level of expectation for all schools. Education is not only more complicated than this, and less responsive to scientific analysis. There is also a significant and unresolved debate about what the desired outcomes are. Is it a set number of higher grade passes at GCSE? Is it a job? Is it a mature and fully-rounded adult? Is it a love of learning? 'Scientific analysis can tell you what is the case in a very systematic and rational manner, but it cannot tell you what ought to be the case' (Bottery, 1992, p. 27).

One experience of target-setting that we do have in education is that of performance-related pay (PRP) for heads and deputies. Fitz-Gibbon (1996) has raised important questions about the effectiveness of this. As she points out, the School Teachers' Review Body itself (p. 2) recognized that PRP generally might be divisive, demotivating for those missing out, likely to focus on simplistic, quantitative measures, complicated and time-consuming to administer. There is also a question as to how many schools even acknowledge operating PRP for heads and deputies as they must according to the regulations — estimates are as low as 30 per cent. It seems likely that governing bodies find it difficult to turn down an award to a 'pushy' head, even though it is at the expense of other parts of the school budget; while a conscientious head who is anxious about the poverty of the school's resources will suffer. There is a worry that only the wealthier schools will take advantage of a broader application of PRP, and that this will widen the already large gap between rich and poor schools. PRP for senior management is also founded on a paradox. The head and deputies themselves are usually responsible for collecting and reporting the data that the governing body will use to determine whether or not an award will be made. As Fitz-Gibbon points out: 'It is strange that there is a *negative* view of people as being motivated only by pay, along with total *positive* faith in their willingness to turn in poor indicators of their own performance' (p. 191).

Certainly, again, there is absence of evidence to show that pay incentives work: 'The mythology is that superior US corporate performance is greatly stimulated by stock options, cash-incentive awards, and the like. But studies done before these goodies became all but universal revealed, among the top 100 US companies, no distinction in results between managements that granted themselves every financial stimulus under the sun and those tiny few that bumbled along on straight salary — except that, by performing no better than the straight-salary managers, the carrot-danglers got much richer . . . incentive awards, unanswerably, seem to have no discernible incentive effect' (Heller, 1995, pp. 135–7).

A Target of Quality?

Much of industry has moved on a great deal since Frederick Taylor's day. Modern thinking on quality has been defined largely by the work of W Edwards Deming (see, for example, Deming, 1982). Deming's work being unappreciated in the United States after the Second World War, he moved to Japan, where his ideas were probably one of the major factors in the eventual world domination of the motor industry. Despite Deming's background as a statistician, the emphasis in his work is on the worker's responsibility for quality assurance, and the need to 'beware of figures': 'Measures of productivity do not lead to improvement in productivity' (ibid, p. 15). Deming's recipe for quality was to give the system back to the people who operate it: 'Cease dependence on inspection to achieve quality. Eliminate the need for inspection on a mass basis by building quality into the product in the first place. . . . the bulk of the causes of low quality and low productivity belong to the system and thus lie beyond the power of the work force . . . Eliminate management by objective. Eliminate management by numbers, numerical goals. Substitute leadership.' (ibid, pp. 23–4). Deming worked largely in the production industry, but his ideas are clearly transferable, because they are so people- and learning-centred: 'Nobody can enjoy learning if he must constantly be concerned about his rating on the job. No child can enjoy learning if he must constantly be concerned about grading and gold stars for his performance' (Neave, 1990, p. 278).

Our obsession with results starts in the infant school. While an element of reward may be appropriate for all learners, there is a danger in overplaying the extrinsic rewards awarded by teachers only apparently for good performance. Smiley faces, merit points and golden time may be seen as rewards for good performance, but even very young children know that the judgments made by teachers are very subjective and very relative. A harsher view might be that they are sheer bribery — a fact acknowledged by the children who refuse to play in a competition they see themselves as unable to win — and by the children who reject the system in favour of a more exciting competition for demerits. All extrinsic rewards run the risk of detracting from the pleasure of doing the task for its own sake — what Deming calls 'joy in work'.

Service industries and education do need some information about numbers. But their major source of quality assessment could be surveys of customer/user satisfaction. For this, we need to know more about the consumer's expectations. What do parents (and pupils themselves) want out of school? It is not all the same thing though, because they focus on those things which can be counted, official sources seem to suggest that it is. If we think schools are complicated systems, consider the hotel industry instead.

Why do people stay in hotels? Some of the customer opinion cards recognize that there are many reasons. It might be to stop over on a journey; to stay for a holiday; to go for a job interview; or to have a secret rendezvous, or a whole host of other reasons. If such a simple activity can be so complicated, how much more complicated must be the motivations for parents to ensure that their children go to school, and their expectations of what it will give them. Some exploration of motivation is essential to measure satisfaction.

We shall look at quality issues in schools in more detail in chapter 10.

A World Without Targets? Observation and Information Improve Performance Without the Need for Targets

It has been suggested (e.g. in Fitz-Gibbon, 1996, p. 195, and by Deming, 1982) that information *by itself* may improve performance. Feedback motivates. Knowing how we are doing compared to our past performance or compared to the performance of others, should provide sufficient incentive to do better. If we are doing not so well, we are spurred on to do better. If we are doing well, we are encouraged to do even better. Externally-set targets remove the sense of reward from our own control. In schools, we have not had the chance to find out whether or not this works. Information — and questionable information at that — has been inextricably linked with performance tables. Indeed, as we have seen, between 1996 and 1998 Ofsted *would not* release accurate information, on the grounds that its own less scientific judgments might be undermined. This has resulted in information being associated with fear rather than enlightenment. While politicians are said to use statistics as a drunk uses a lamp-post — for support rather than for illumination; so Ofsted and the DfEE have used the publication of school 'results' as a psychopath uses a walking stick — to beat you with, rather than to help him move forward.

What Sort of Targets Are There?

None of the arguments put forward invalidates the use of targets in schools. But they do raise serious questions about how governing bodies should go about implementing the DfEE regulations and LEA suggestions for target-setting. Now that we have considered some of the problems associated with the measurement of schools and children, we need to look at the different kinds of targets we might use in schools.

We have already established that measurements, and therefore target-setting:

- are complex;
- need to support improvement rather than label and reinforce failure;
- need to address *all* the processes which are thought to be worthwhile.

The application of targets is founded upon a set of performance indicators which are agreed as accurate definitions of what a school wants to be and to do. The performance indicator is a criterion against which current achievement is measured and future performance targetted.

There are three ways in which we can look at the performance of the school, how it is indicated, and how the targets are formulated. How we decide which to use is determined by our view of the school's purpose:

1 HOW we measure performance.
2 WHERE we measure performance.
3 WHAT sort of performance we measure.

HOW We Measure Performance

This is the only concern of the DfEE booklets published to help schools in the setting of targets (DfEE, 1997b and 1997c). They suggest three ways of measuring pupil attainment. We can use *threshold* targets — stating a level we want all children to achieve, and measuring the proportion of children who actually achieve it. This is how 'results' have been published for both primary and secondary schools, and threshold scores are an important gauge by which Ofsted decides the acceptability of a school's performance. The principal scores are expressed as:

- the proportion of children achieving Level 2 or above at the end of Key Stage 1 in English and mathematics;
- the proportion of children achieving Level 4 or above at the end of Key Stage 2 in English, mathematics and science;
- the proportion of children achieving Level 5 or above at the end of Key Stage 3 in English, mathematics and science;

- the proportion of children achieving five or more higher grade GCSEs, and the proportion of children achieving one or more GCSE grades A to G, at the end of Key Stage 4.

The weakness of such threshold targets has been seen above. The decision on the level desired, or expected, is critical. Too high — and too many fail. Too low — and too many succeed. Failure, of course, is built in. The system doesn't work unless the 'right' proportion of children, and therefore schools, fail. If too few fail, we are told (*pace* Ofsted, 1998a) that the standard is too low. If too many fail, we are told that teaching standards are too low. Presumably, as more pass the target level year by year, the level will be raised. Thus what is presented as an objective, criterion-referenced test becomes norm-referenced by the application of a pass/fail line.

Threshold targets also have the built-in weakness of tempting schools to focus their efforts on the children likely to fall just short of the level. If, for example, we were organizing the Grand National, we might be anxious to increase the proportion of horses successfully getting over Becher's Brook by a certain time. We would, of course, be foolish to spend any time on the horses that are already approaching the following jump. Similarly, it would be wasted effort to stand by the previous jump cheering on, or whipping, the horses that cannot possibly make the distance in time. We need to be expending all our efforts on those horses approaching Becher's and, if necessary, getting behind them and helping to push them over.

Schools that adopt this approach end up targetting those children who are predicted to fall on or just short of the critical performance measure, Level 2 at Key Stage 1, Level 4 at KS2, five higher grade GCSEs. Of necessity, other pupils will be comparatively neglected, whether they are under- or over-achievers. A DfEE publication cites as an example a school where 'A major task was to identify pupils on the C–D borderline, and to mentor them' (DfEE, 1996a, p. 32).

Threshold targets *by themselves* may foster such discriminatory practices. Some primary headteachers have been honest enough to admit that they and their staff do concentrate on such children, and will continue to do so while those are the results by which schools are publicly compared. All but one of the DfEE targets are threshold targets, despite its own admission (DfEE, 1997b, p. 13) that 'the school is likely to give more attention to high performing pupils, and to those just falling short of the threshold'. It would be difficult not to see a link between the growing importance of league tables for secondary schools based on the proportion of pupils achieving five higher grades at GCSE, and the unprecedented increase in the gap between the attainment of abler pupils and the number of failures in maths and English, which happened in the summer of 1998. In that year, the pass rate at grades A–C went up by 0.3 per cent to 54.7 per cent — the tenth increase in a row since the introduction of GCSEs. At the same time, the proportion failing to get a pass at grade G or above increased from 1.5 per cent to 2.3 per cent. In maths, the failure rate more than doubled to 5.2 per cent. In English, the pass rate at the higher grades rose from 56 to 56.5 per cent, while those failing to get a grade G or above doubled from 0.5 per cent to 1 per cent.

Average targets at least hold out the promise of more equable treatment. Improving average GCSE scores, or average performance at the end of Key Stage 2, suggests that improvement in the attainment of *all* pupils is equally important. However, averages can also be improved by focusing on small groups of children to the comparative neglect of others.

Reliability targets are guarantees of minimum entitlement. Every child may be guaranteed to achieve Level 3 at KS2, or staff ensure that no children leave without at least one GCSE. A combination of average and reliability targets may ensure that children of all abilities receive equal attention.

WHERE We Measure Performance

All DfEE targets focus on the *outputs* of schooling — the tests and examinations that pupils pass at different levels, one of which at each stage is designated as the 'expected' level.

There are, however, other stages in the delivery of education — the input, the process and the long-term outcome, as well as the short-term output. Elements of each of these stages may be defined in terms of a performance indicator, may be measurable, and therefore may be the subject of a target. These stages are shown in figure 3.1. These four elements of school activity can all be the subject of targets, and will be explored further in the following chapters.

WHAT We Measure

All the targets required by the DfEE are *quantity* targets — they come about through counting current outputs and projecting future, hoped-for, numerical scores. The measurement that happens involves counting some result that can have numbers attached to it, even where the counting may be of something that is subjective and comparatively unscientific, such as user satisfaction. It is possible, however, to have *quality* targets. While these may not be as 'scientific', they may get closer to accurately recording people's experiences of a service organization such as a school. We will look at quality issues and targets (usually expressed as quality *standards*) in chapter 10.

If schooling is for all our children and all our society, we must beware of the quasi-scientific approach to school improvement which dominates the educational literature and the political debate. School effectiveness research efforts 'cloak school practices in a progressive, social-darwinist, eugenic rationale. It is progressive because it seeks more efficient and effective ways of steering social progress. It is social-darwinist because it accepts survival of the fittest.

And it is eugenic because it privileges the desirable and seeks to eliminate the negative' (Hamilton, 1998, p. 13).

Do schools have to be like this? Is it the task of governing bodies to count scores and demand outputs? Or is there a more appropriate way for governors to set about the critical job of determining what schools should be doing?

How It Might Be

Schools, through their governing bodies, may commit themselves to a much broader range of target-setting than is required — provided that they simultaneously recognize a different definition and purpose of target-setting. Targets, or promises, or guarantees, performance indicators or quality standards can help a school identify what is *really* important to it — what reflects its own values, and its own expectations and aspirations for its pupils. They can help to find ways to answer the fundamental question that governing bodies should be asking: 'How do we know *how* our school is doing?'

The process, offered as something of an antidote to the planning processes offered elsewhere, might be something like this:

1 **Deciding what matters**
    Deciding what is important — what inputs, processes, outputs and outcomes are vital for the pupils of this school: 'Parental and educational opinion unite in regarding all-round development towards maturity as a target of no less importance than attainment in any one subject or any agreed common core of subjects. General development therefore needs to be recorded and assessed with no less attention than is given to attainment in the various basic skills with which a school concerns itself.' (Hopkinson, 1978, p. 13)

2 **Describing what matters**
    How can 'what matters' best be expressed in terms which describe clearly what children should be doing and be able to do?

3 **Asking what matters**
    How can the pupils, parents and staff (and the wider community) be involved in determining the school's aims and targets, so that there is a sense of ownership over not just the activities of the school, but over the school itself?

4 **Measuring what matters**
    How can the school express improvement or progress towards a desired end — by counting? Or otherwise? B W Kay (1978, pp. 29–30) identifies six areas of pupil performance which might be used as the basis for assessment: Verbal, mathematical, scientific, ethical, aesthetic, physical: 'Any assessment must be based on some sort of sampling, and the items tested can only be a tiny proportion of those present in the school curriculum. It is important that they should be the most

significant, *even though it is likely that the most significant will often be the most difficult to assess'* (p. 30).

5 **Telling people how we're doing**

Expressing the school's priorities and guarantees in terms of targets is a much more direct way of communicating the school's mission than through rhetorical declamation or complex development plans. A series of simple statements, with comments on progress towards them, will make it clear to pupils and parents what the school's values are. For pupils and staff, giving such information may be enough in itself to motivate them. The targets themselves become redundant.

This approach is less utilitarian, more respectful and caring of people. Targets for schools need not be a process of putting arrows in a board. Targets which are put together in this way have failure built in. The whole point of playing darts is that not everyone scores treble 20 all the time. The process of achieving targets should not be a quest for the perfection defined by someone else, because such a quest can never be realized. Such targets cause only frustration. Targets should rather resemble the ripples that flow out from a stone thrown into the middle of a pond. Everyone will be affected, more or less, just as all the surface of the water is affected. But of course most of the movement in the water — the real and lasting changes that people experience — happens under the surface.

Part II

Leading a Quality School

This section of the book considers how the governing body can set targets which enhance the quality of learning for all the pupils. To make the exercise more manageable, the work of the governing body has been divided into a number of areas. These are the ones which are usually given to committees or working parties to consider in more detail. Governing bodies find their own best committee and working party structures, and this book does not mean to recommend the pattern used here. It does seem to be the most common although, inevitably, there is some overlap in the areas of responsibility.

The targets are input, process, output and outcome targets (see figure 3.1 on page 24 for a clarification of these terms). Some are quantity targets, some quality — again, the distinction is not always clear. Some are high-level targets affecting all the work of the school. Others are low-level, short-term and may appear marginal. They *all* affect the quality of learning and teaching, however indirectly.

Each chapter in this section opens with a brief survey of the area of responsibility, and of how a committee or working party of governors might go about the work. The assumptions are that:

(i)   every committee or working party has clear terms of reference (for model terms of reference see, for example, Arden, 1998);

(ii)   they all approach their task by setting targets which reflect the priorities of the governing body;

(iii)   all targets have been negotiated with staff (and pupils and parents and others where appropriate);

(iv)   high-level targets are key issues in the school development/ improvement plan, and have been agreed by the whole governing body;

(v)   each target has a plan attached to it showing how it is to be achieved. A model is shown in table 4.1;

(vi)   the principal task of the governing body and committee meetings is for staff and governors — mainly the head — to report on the progress made towards targets, so emphasizing the governing body's role in monitoring;

(vii) the governing body has a cycle of planning — monitoring — evaluating (described in Gann, 1998) which provides the framework for this process.

Most of the targets listed in the following chapters have been proposed by serving governors. Many have been adopted by schools. Others are proposed by the DfEE, LEAs and other publications. They are offered as a starting point for governing body debate — not to be adopted *en bloc*, or even used as a 'menu'. Neither does this pretend to be an exhaustive list — more of an appetizer to get discussion started. Schools will consider very carefully how many targets at different levels they can realistically manage at one time. However, target-setting in one sense is not a new experience for achools. For many schools, the targets they adopt will merely be a formalization of the aims and objectives, priorities and principles they have had in place for some years.

As we have seen, the DfEE requires two or three targets as a minimum, depending on the Key Stages taught. Some LEAs suggest more (and some LEAs put pressure on schools to adopt more). A school may agree 50 or more. More likely, the school's targets will be agreed by a cumulative process, in which the values of the school and its community are constantly being interpreted and reinterpreted by the governors and staff. Some will be permanent, such as quality standards. Some will be long-term. All will be reviewed annually, at which point some will be revised. Each governing body will have its own procedure. But all the targets adopted will reflect the priorities of the governors, their expectations of the children, and their aspirations for them.

Chapter 4

Target-setting in the Curriculum

What the Curriculum Is

The word 'curriculum' is often used narrowly as synonymous with the programmes of study in the core and foundation subjects. However, it can also
describe the whole sum of school activities — intentional and unintentional —
not just the explicitly didactic bits in the classroom. Educationists have created
libraries of books which consider what the curriculum is, and this is not the
place to review that literature. Instead, for our purposes, curriculum will be
defined in its widest sense — everything that is meant to happen in the school.

This holistic view of the curriculum raises the question of what the curriculum is for — and what schools are for. This has been addressed by Barber
(1996), whose influence as Head of the Standards and Effectiveness Unit at
the DfEE is considerable — see table 4.2. School governors need to debate
the balance of these traditions within their own school curriculum. This will
enable them to forge the school's distinctive approach to learning, as they are
required to do.

If the curriculum is everything that happens within the school experience,
governors have the potential for exercising a critical influence. For the first few
years after the 1988 Act, many governing bodies fought shy of dealing with
curriculum matters. As Joan Sallis — a trainer of governors and member of
the influential Taylor Committee of the 1970s — says, many governing bodies
have a preference for 'looking into lavatories rather than looking into learning'
(quoted in Earley and Creese, 1998). However, when confronted with their
responsibilities, a group of governors in a development workshop compiled
the following list of their responsibilities, as representing some of the key areas
where governing body policy-making defines the school:

1   Curriculum Policy
2   Sex Education
3   Drugs/Smoking Policy
4   Health and Safety Policy
5   Special Needs — ensuring compliance with the Code of Practice
6   School Trips
7   Behaviour and Discipline
8   Staffing
9   School Development Plan

Table 4.1 Action planning

KEY ISSUE	WHERE DO WE WANT TO BE?	HOW WILL WE GET THERE?	BY WHEN?	WHAT WILL WE NEED?	HOW WILL WE KNOW WHEN WE HAVE ARRIVED?	LEADER: MONITOR:
	Objectives	Steps to be taken	Target Dates	Resources	Success Criteria	

Table 4.2 Four traditions of the curriculum

Exponents of **[the liberal–humanist tradition]** would argue that . . . western thought has developed a sophisticated understanding of people and the universe which they inhabit. This understanding is divided into a series of disciplines such as science and philosophy, which examine specific aspects of human experience and which have developed their own traditions and approaches to explaining the world and arriving at the true, the good and the beautiful . . . The aim of the school curriculum, in the liberal–humanist view, is to introduce pupils to each form of thought or 'community of discourse'.

The progressive tradition, by contrast, places the child at the centre of the educational process. In this view, the purpose of education is to unlock the potential of the child. The child will be offered a range of experiences and opportunities through which to discover the world; learning will be an active process of discovery; and the process of learning is considered at least as important if not more so than the product or outcome. In this tradition the curriculum is therefore best viewed as a set of opportunities or experiences, rather than a clearly defined set of knowledge or skills. Teaching becomes a facilitative process and opportunistic in the sense of responding to the needs of individual pupils as they become apparent.

A third tradition is **the technocratic tradition**. This is an approach to curriculum design which assumes that the curriculum can be set down in specific objectives or outcomes. Once these are established it is possible to work back from them and to work out how to achieve them. Assessment, in this approach, involves testing whether pupils have achieved the specified objectives.

The final tradition to be identified here is **the cultural–analysis tradition** . . . In this view the chief task of the schools is to transmit elements of a culture from one generation to the next. The curriculum . . . is seen as a cultural artefact which emerges from a social negotiation between generations. (Barber, 1996, pp. 10–14)

10 Curriculum Enhancement
11 Parental Involvement
12 Budget
13 The Teaching Environment
14 Horizontal/Vertical Grouping
15 Team Teaching
16 Mixed Ability/Setting/Streaming
17 Lunchtime Supervision
18 Discrimination/Equal Opportunities
19 Uniform
20 Reading Schemes/'Real Books'
21 Balance in the Curriculum
22 Local and Community Aspects
23 Collective Worship
24 Exam/Test Results
25 Political Balance
26 Charging Policy
27 Lesson Times/School Day Times
28 Information Technology

29 Ethos
30 Extra-curricular Activities
31 Teaching/Learning Styles
32 Receiving Complaints re the Curriculum
33 Ensuring Premises are 'Fit for Purpose'

What Governing Bodies Have to Do

Governing bodies must:

- set the aims of the curriculum in the unique circumstances of the school;
- consider and adopt (and if appropriate modify) the LEA curriculum policy (or decide the curriculum policy in non-LEA-maintained schools);
- determine the staffing of the school to ensure that it is able to deliver the curriculum;
- ensure that the curriculum is meeting the needs of *all* the pupils.

In addition to ensuring that the school meets statutory requirements in the delivery and assessment of the curriculum, the governing body must monitor pupils' progress, using target-setting and benchmarking. Ofsted inspectors have used the following list to ensure that a school's curriculum complies with the law. They will check that it:

- is balanced and broadly based, promotes pupils' intellectual, physical and personal development and prepares pupils for the next stage of education, training or employment;
- meets statutory requirements to teach the subjects of the National Curriculum, religious education and sex education, where these apply;
- provides equality of access and opportunity for pupils to learn and make progress;
- meets the curricular requirements of all pupils on the school's Code of Practice special educational needs register;
- is planned effectively, providing continuity and progression of learning;
- is enriched by extra-curricular provision, including sport;
- includes, for pupils of secondary age, careers education and impartial guidance, drawing on the careers service;

and in relation to assessment, the extent to which:

- there are effective systems for assessing pupils' attainment;
- assessment information is used to inform curriculum planning (Ofsted, 1995, p. 78).

To know that all this is happening is potentially a difficult job for a predominantly lay governing body. At least, much of the 'educational establishment'

Figure 4.1 *CURRICULUM: An example of the division of responsibilities between the governing body and the headteacher*

The headteacher:

draws up the school curriculum plan within the overall statutory framework and the policy framework set by the governing body;

ensures its implementation;

is responsible for day to day decisions on the curriculum.

The governing body:

determines a policy for delivering a broad and balanced curriculum within the statutory framework in consultation with the headteacher, including a policy on sex education;

satisfies itself that requirements for the delivery and assessment of the National Curriculum are being met and that religious education is being provided;

ensures that appropriate monitoring arrangements are in place and that outcomes are being evaluated through reports from the headteacher.

would like to make out that discharging these monitoring duties is something only 'professional educationists' can do. Certainly, this was an area reserved for the teaching profession until 1976, when Prime Minister Callaghan's Ruskin College speech (see above, page 16) put the accountability cat among the establishment pigeons. Even then, another 10 years passed before the politicians decisively wrested control over curriculum content from their hands. So is there a place for 'ordinary' lay governors in the debate? While there are some jobs that only professionals can do — the teaching, the monitoring of individual and group learning, the matching of activities to aims and objectives, and so on — there is an overall strategic role for governors who represent the community ownership of a school. Monitoring the curriculum is a task which requires the skills and knowledge of the professional to be balanced by governing body control of the aims and objectives themselves. There is an example of the division of responsibilities between the governing body and the headteacher over the curriculum given in *Guidance on Good Governance* (DfEE, 1996b), and shown in figure 4.1. (A revised and updated edition of the Guidance is to be published in 1999.)

In fact, most of the words used to describe the curriculum are perfectly good 'lay' words. They have meanings which any intelligent person can grasp, interrogate and identify. There are, of course, 'official' explanations aplenty, with (regularly changing) policy statements of what the DfEE and Ofsted understand by the terms. But the laypersons' grasp of the word will allow them to interrogate the staff, to ask for evidence, and to satisfy themselves of the presence of that characteristic.

Governors must ensure that the school curriculum displays certain characteristics. First, it must show *breadth* — that is, they must ensure that every child comes into contact with all areas of learning.

Coupled with the idea of breadth is that of *balance* — that each area of learning is given the appropriate attention.

Breadth and balance must be the two basic components of a curriculum plan. Neither of these is a difficult concept. You do not have to be a professional educator to understand either, or to recognize either. Of course, as with every other area of the school's work, governors will be dependent on professionals to interpret, explain and demonstrate these characteristics within the school. Where the permanent staff need help to do this, they will call in subject specialists, inspectors and advisers. But the ideas are sufficiently penetrable by lay people for them to be able to monitor the staff's delivery of them.

There are other important characteristics which a school curriculum must display, although the interpretation of them by the professionals may vary slightly from year to year. These are *relevance*, that the curriculum must be appropriate to pupils' needs. This suggests, of course, that pupils' needs will differ from community to community, and therefore that the curriculum will be marginally — or in some cases significantly — different in each school. The curriculum must also be *differentiated* — that is, it must cater for pupils of a range of abilities in the tasks given to them, and in the outcomes expected of them.

The curriculum must also show *progression* and *continuity.* The pupils should be able to make sense of the range of experiences offered to them throughout the day, the week, the month and the year. Learning is to some extent cumulative, and pupils should be able to build their knowledge in a sequential way — while allowing for the fact that much learning is haphazard and unexpected.

These six key words provide a platform from which governors can explore the curriculum offered by the school in rather more depth than by the single question: 'Are we meeting statutory requirements?'. Monitoring will happen through the committee's interrogation of staff, by visits to departments and classrooms, by shadowing pupils, by attachment to an area of the school's work. All of these methods involve the governors in asking questions, in learning about the impact of their policies and procedures on the curriculum. They are not inspections, because lay governors do not have the expertise to inspect. They are, rather, a form of quality *assurance*, where the governors determine 'the standards, appropriate methods and quality requirements', and then examine 'the extent to which practices meet these standards' (Murgatroyd and Morgan, 1993, p. 45). They are not quality *control*, which is about checking and inspecting. That is a job for the professionals.

Understanding the six key words is not the same as understanding the way all learning happens. What is described above are the characteristics of the curriculum which, at the present time, seems to be most effective for most pupils, as some experts believe. It may not always be the case. Beliefs and traditions change, as we have seen over the last forty years alone. The current curriculum tradition will not always be in the ascendancy. As with every other idea, fashion and movement in education, school governors will work with what they must in order to meet the latest statutory requirements, or with the

most up-to-date thinking of the latest director of Ofsted or local chief education officer. The governing body will then temper this with their own common
sense and experience, and with the knowledge and experience of the staff
who advise them.

To help governors approach the issues raised by this list of characteristics
required of the school curriculum, they might ask themselves the following
questions. This will, if necessary, lift the governing body debate on to a plane
more appropriate to the strategic role:

1   What requirements should the school have of all its students?
In one secondary school in a remote rural area, changes in senior staff and the
governing body triggered questions about the cultural breadth of pupils' background experiences. Pupils achieving high grade exam passes were ignorant
of their geographical surroundings, of the arts and politics. Many had never
spent a night away from their parents. The school determined some short-term
targets for all pupils — first, that all pupils would have a residential experience
by the end of their first year. To enable the school timetable to cope with this,
a series of days was organized where pupils could make (limited, and sometimes guided) choices of activity on and off site. Visits were arranged for whole
year groups to theatres and cinemas, museums and so on. The targets were
process targets, the aim was to send pupils out from the school with a much
wider experience of the world. The process target was simple to measure,
the outcome target more difficult.

2   What opportunities should be offered to all pupils?
In the same school, very few pupils had been abroad. Traditionally the school
had offered a European trip with a lot of watersports. This was popular with
staff, and with the small minority of parents who could afford the substantial
cost. The school changed its priorities, to offer a French trip to all its year 7
pupils at a very low cost. The trip concentrated on offering new cultural experiences to the children, living with a French family, having to make purchases
in shops and cafes and so on. The school set a target of getting all pupils to
have a residential experience abroad by the end of year 8. Again, a process
target was easy to measure.

3   What choices should be offered to pupils?
Pupils need to exercise choice from their earliest days in school. Often, the
arena for such choices in infant schools is not first and foremost the classroom.
It may be the dining hall, where children are helped by lunchtime supervisors
in choosing their lunches. Choices are offered in activities, when tasks have
been completed. Choices not only enrich the curriculum, but also develop
children's independence and sense of individuality and self-worth.

4   What support should be offered to pupils?
While requirements and choices may ensure breadth and balance, appropriate
arrangements for support to all pupils will ensure differentiation. This means

Figure 4.2   Half-termly letter

Dear Parents,

After Christmas the children in reception will be working on a topic based around children's stories. Below is a list of those stories, the letter of the week and some other information:

Week Beginning:
5 Jan — *The Hungry Caterpillar.* Please could the children bring in an old sock and a couple of buttons to make a caterpillar.

12 Jan — Letter of the week is 'g'. The children can bring in things beginning with that letter.

19 Jan — *Goldilocks and the Three Bears.* The children can bring in a bear from home, labelled, to put on a class display. If you have any books about bears we would love to use them! The letter of the week is 'o'.

26 Jan — The letter of the week is 'f'. During this week the children will be tasting different cereals and porridge. If your child has any food allergies please let his/her class teacher know.

2 Feb — *The Three Billy Goats Gruff.* During this week the children will be walking over the Itchen bridge before making their own. If you have any old photos or books about the bridge please can we borrow them! The letter for this week is 'p'.

9 Feb — The letter of the week is 'k'. This half-term ends on Friday 13.

If you can spare any time after Christmas to come in and help it would be much appreciated!

We look forward to seeing you all in the new term,

support for the lower attaining child and for the higher attainer too. It suggests that the governing body should consider the resources available to all children, and 'extra-curricular' provision, such as access to the library and homework clubs. It may imply that different kinds of support need to be available, and it may suggest some positive discrimination towards some groups.

5   What information should be given to pupils?

The rhetoric of parent–school partnership has not been supported by real and useful information about what children are going to do in school. However, it takes little effort to ensure that pupils of all ages, and parents of pupils of all ages, know their broad programmes of study in advance, so that families can support learning. Some good practice can now be seen in primary schools. An example of a simple half-termly letter from an infant school is shown in figure 4.2. Information such as this is not threatening or demanding, but allows families to support the learning as far as they are able. As pupils progress, information might include recommendations of reading, discussion points, videos or visits that the family can make together. It allows the beginning of a real partnership without coercion or unrealistic expectations.

These five questions enable governors to get to grips with the features of their school's curriculum and to provide a lay view, balanced by the professional advice and experience of the teaching staff.

In addition governing bodies will need all the information provided by the Qualifications and Curriculum Authority (e.g. in the school's PANDA reports, and in publications such as 'Standards at Key Stage 1; Year 4; Key Stage 2; Key Stage 3' published annually).

SOME EXAMPLES OF TARGETS IN THE CURRICULUM

Input Targets
The school meets statutory requirements in the delivery and assessment of the curriculum:
(Quotes from Ofsted, 1995, are from the Guidance on Inspection — page numbers are quoted from the version for secondary schools but are also in the versions for primary and special schools)

- The curriculum meets statutory requirements to teach the subjects of the National Curriculum, religious education and sex education, where these apply (p. 78).
- The governing body is monitoring pupil progress.
- The curriculum displays breadth — all pupils come into contact with all areas of learning.
- The curriculum displays balance — each area of learning is given appropriate attention.
- The curriculum is relevant to the needs of all pupils.
- The curriculum displays different kinds of provision for each pupil.
- The curriculum displays progression for all pupils.
- The curriculum displays continuity for all pupils.
- The curriculum promotes pupils' intellectual, physical and personal development and prepares pupils for the next stage of education, training or employment (ibid).
- The curriculum provides equality of access and opportunity for pupils to learn and to make progress (ibid).
- The curriculum meets the requirements of all pupils on the school's Code of Practice special educational needs register (ibid).
- The curriculum is planned effectively (ibid).
- The curriculum is enriched by extra-curricular provision, including sport (ibid).
- The curriculum includes, for pupils of secondary age, careers education and impartial guidance, drawing on the careers service (ibid).
- There are effective systems for assessing pupils' attainment (ibid).
- Assessment information is used to inform curriculum planning (ibid).

- The governing body has agreed and published, and regularly reviews, the aims of the curriculum.
- The governing body has considered and adopted (and, if desired, modified) its curriculum policy, where required in line with the local authority's policy.
- The governing body determines a policy for delivering a broad and balanced curriculum within the statutory framework in consultation with the headteacher (DfEE, 1996b, p. 7).
- The headteacher draws up a school curriculum plan within the overall statutory framework and the policy framework set by the governing body (ibid).
- The headteacher ensures the implementation of the curriculum plan and reports on it to the governing body (ibid).
- The governing body ensures that appropriate monitoring arrangements are in place and that outcomes are being evaluated through reports from the headteacher (ibid).
- The governing body has determined the level and composition of staffing within the school.
- The governing body ensures that the curriculum meets the needs of all pupils.
- The curriculum promotes the spiritual, moral, cultural, mental and physical development of pupils (Ofsted, 1995, p. 79).
- The curriculum prepares pupils for the opportunities, responsibilities and experiences of adult life (ibid).
- The school provides health education, including education about drug misuse (ibid).

In addition:
- Appropriate opportunities for choice are provided for all pupils.
- Appropriate support is provided for all pupils.
- Appropriate information about the curriculum, syllabuses and schemes of work is given to pupils and parents.
- Teacher assessments of pupils' attainment at the end of Key Stage tests will fall within x per cent of test results.
- A satisfaction questionnaire will be delivered to all pupils once a year, covering areas such as learning outcomes, social aspects of the school, safety, confidence, enjoyment, values.
- The governing body will agree patterns of rewards and sanctions used withn the school, and receive reports on their use by year and by department/subject area/class.

- Extra-curricular activities will be offered to all pupils after school/during lunchtimes on x days a week throughout the year.
- The range of extra-curricular activities will include academic, social, cultural and physical activities.
- The size of classes will not exceed x.

Process Targets

- The proportion of (boys/girls) pupils participating in all extra-curricular activities will be x per cent.
- The proportion of year X pupils participating in extra-curricular activities will be x per cent.
- All pupils will participate in a school visit with two nights away from home during year X.
- All pupils will have at least one hour's swimming lessons during year X.
- All pupils will spend at least x hours per week with exclusive access to a computer.
- All pupils will spend at least x hours each week working cooperatively in small groups.
- All pupils will spend at least x hours each week engaged in literacy-related work.
- All pupils will spend at least x hours each week engaged in numeracy-related work.
- All pupils will be introduced to the rudiments of foreign language work during year X.

Output Targets

Government Targets for the year 2002:
Foundation Targets:

- By age 19, 85 per cent of young people to achieve five GCSEs at grade C or above, an intermediate GNVQ or an NVQ Level 2 (currently at about 72 per cent).
- By age 19, 75 per cent of young people to achieve Level 2 competence in communication, numeracy and information technology, and 35 per cent to achieve Level 3 by age 21.
- By age 21, 60 per cent of young people to achieve two GCE Advanced levels, an Advanced GNVQ or an NVQ Level 3 (currently about 50 per cent).

Lifetime Targets:

- 50 per cent of the workforce to be qualified to NVQ Level 3, Advanced GNVQ or two GCE A level standard (currently about 42 per cent).
- 28 per cent of the workforce to have a vocational, professional, management or academic qualification at NVQ Level 4 or above (currently about 25 per cent).
- 70 per cent of all organizations employing 200+, and 45 per cent of those employing 50+, to be recognized as Investors in People (though only 22 per cent and 10 per cent respectively, this is expected to be met on current commitments). *(Sources: DfEE, QCA and Ofsted, 1997; NACETT, 1998)*

For the year 2002:

- At the end of Key Stage 2, 80 per cent of 11-year-olds will achieve Level 4 or above in English.
- At the end of Key Stage 2, 75 per cent of 11-year-olds will achieve Level 4 or above in mathematics. *(These targets have been extrapolated for individual LEAs)*

Mandatory School Targets:

- At the end of Key Stage 2, the percentage of pupils attaining Level 4 or above in English will be . . .
- At the end of Key Stage 2, the percentage of pupils attaining Level 4 or above in mathematics will be . . .
- At the end of Key Stage 4, the percentage of pupils attaining five or more GCSEs or equivalent at grades A–C will be . . .
- At the end of Key Stage 4, the percentage of pupils attaining 1 or more GCSEs or equivalent at grades A–G will be . . .
- At the end of Key Stage 4, the average GCSE or equivalent points score per pupil will be . . . *(Targets will have to be set each autumn term, starting in 1998, and relating to those pupils taking National Curriculum tests or GCSE examinations or equivalent towards the end of the following school year i.e. five terms later)* *(Source: DfEE, 1998b)*

Additional School Targets:

- All pupils will add two levels to their performance between Key Stage 2 at 11 and Key Stage 3 at age 14.

- All pupils will add two levels to their performance between Key Stage 3 at 14 and Key Stage 4 at age 16.
- Targets for numbers or proportions achieving levels (say, Level 3, or graded levels within Level 2 in reading) at end of Key Stage 1, or average scores at end of Key Stage 1, in reading, writing, mathematics.
- Targets for numbers or proportions achieving levels (say, Level 5) at end of Key Stage 2, or average scores at end of Key Stage 2, in English, mathematics and science.
- Targets for numbers or proportions achieving levels at end of Key Stage 3, or average scores at end of Key Stage 3, in English, mathematics and science.
- The proportion of pupils achieving at least GCSE grade C in English, mathematics and science.
- The proportion of pupils achieving at least GCSE grade G in English, mathematics and science, individually and collectively.
- The proportion of boys achieving the above levels at the four Key Stages.
- The proportion of girls achieving the above levels at the four Key Stages.
- The proportion of pupils of minority ethnic origin, or with English as a second language, achieving the above levels at the four Key Stages.
- The proportion of pupils from different neighbourhoods within the school catchment area achieving the above levels at the four Key Stages.
- The difference between the achievements of different groups of pupils within the school — by gender, ethnic origin, social class, residence, and other relevant categories.
- The proportion of positive responses to a pupil satisfaction survey.
- The equal application of rewards and sanctions across years, classes and subject areas.
- The ratio of rewards given to sanctions applied (say, 3:1).
- The average progress made by pupils will be equivalent to half a NC Level each year. No student will progress at less than half a level each x months.

Outcome Targets

- The proportion of students progressing directly from secondary school to employment, further or higher education will be x per cent.
- The proportion of former students progressing directly to higher education at the age of 18 will be x per cent.
- Pupils will develop a sense of joy in their work.
- Pupils are pleased (though not satisfied) with their achievements.
- Pupils are pleased (though not satisfied) with their attainment.
- Parents are pleased (though not satisfied) with their children's achievements.
- Parents are pleased (though not satisfied) with their children's attainment.

Chapter 5

Targets for the School Environment

Responsibilities

Most schools have a governing body committee dealing with the environment, although this is often called a buildings or premises committee. Environment is favoured here as being a more inclusive term. Ofsted, however, refers to this area of responsibility as 'accommodation':

> Accommodation should be inspected in terms of its adequacy for the numbers on roll and ages of pupils as well as the range of specialist curriculum activities expected of [them]. Coverage should include the arrangements made to use specialist accommodation off-site.
>
> The team should come to a view about the quality of accommodation, including outdoor areas, and whether it provides a stimulating and well-maintained learning environment. (Ofsted, 1995, p. 116)

Ofsted's own evidence (Ofsted, 1998a) suggests that the accommodation in 23 per cent of secondary schools and in 13 per cent of primary schools is inadequate for the delivery of the curriculum. School governors and headteachers will suspect that the true number is far greater. Ofsted (1998c) identifies particular problems in meeting the teaching needs of science, design and technology, art, music and PE. 'Some schools have poor or inaccessible study facilities, including libraries and computer rooms. Some schools are poorly decorated. Some are heavily dependent on temporary accommodation, which can be of poor quality' (ibid, p. 14). While it is difficult to compare schools using different budget heads, it would seem that the average cost of maintenance in locally managed primary and secondary schools is about 1 per cent of the total budget, with expenditure on premises staff taking up a further 1 per cent. This has given governing bodies very little leeway, while most capital funds have been retained by LEAs or handed down for specific approved schemes by other funders.

Nevertheless, the governing body has a significant legal responsibility. It must ensure that the school provides an environment which is 'fit for the purpose' of delivering the school curriculum. As the figures suggest, much of the discussion within committees to which this function has been delegated revolves around priorities to be achieved within a very limited budget. But the key question must be: 'How does the school want to present itself to its pupils, its parents, its staff . . . ?' This is a subsidiary of the key question for governing bodies: 'What is the school for?'

Environment responsibilities are not therefore merely a matter of trying — and more often than not failing — to hold back the tide of demands on the budget. Easier though it is to say than to do, it is a matter of determining the nature of the school's self-presentation, and this does not always have unrealistic resource implications. It may be just as much a matter of reorganizing the use of space, and adding significant touches — a display here, a reception desk there, a hanging basket to soften the entrance area.

The purpose of the school environment might be summed up in three simple phrases. For example:

- to provide an appropriate arena for the delivery of the curriculum;
- to provide a safe, secure and welcoming workplace for pupils and staff;
- to provide an educational, social and leisure resource for the community.

Governing bodies need to avoid the fatalism which often infects them when it comes to matters seemingly so far out of their control. 'Everything that doesn't grow is designed': every design feature of the school environment is their responsibility.

Dangers for the 'Buildings Committee'

If we are not careful, governors' buildings committees can take on a low-level functional role. They can be a haven for people who see themselves as 'only practical', and a place where governors can cause little harm by interfering. Such committees can:

- divorce themselves from 'educational' issues in favour of non-tendentious 'issue-free' practicalities;
- spend and make policy isolated from the governing body;
- provide a comfort-zone for governors intimidated by complex 'professional' issues such as the curriculum and staffing;
- take on inappropriate functions.

A particular danger for such committees is that they, more than any other, will end by 'helping the staff' — which is decidedly not what governors are for. This is a consequence of the underresourcing and lack of expertise of staff. The head and senior staff are unlikely to have much of an investment in being seen as good buildings managers. Similarly, until recently, they had little self-esteem tied up in being effective financial managers. Times are changing, with the management role being recognized by the educational world as embracing every aspect of the school's operations. But it is changing most slowly in the area of environment management.

Therefore, sometimes for perfectly laudable reasons, sometimes for more suspect ones, heads have often been happy to give environment committees a considerable amount of freedom. Sometimes, environment issues serve to let governors with practical backgrounds feel that they are contributing usefully, while heads keep governors concentrating on 'safe' jobs that don't impinge on 'their' own areas — the curriculum and staffing, for example.

Thus it is that buildings committees find themselves doing things which are expected of no other committee: Meeting with LEA officers and contractors to discuss details; inspecting the condition of buildings without professional back-up; making health and safety checks; writing specifications and arranging contract repair and maintenance work. Governors who shrink from entering a classroom because they might have to form a judgment on professional matters will be seen cheerfully prodding plasterwork, clearing drains and counting fire-extinguishers. Not only is this all displacement activity, diverting governors from policy matters. It can lead such governing bodies into taking on legal and moral responsibility which — if they had left things alone — would not be theirs. It is not the governors' job to *do* things, but to ensure that there are systems by which things get done. The people who *do* things are the paid staff, and the advisors, inspectors and consultants we bring in when we need them.

This is not to say that governors — and others — should not offer help to a school when what is needed is some practical expertise or, perhaps, weight of numbers to do a job that would otherwise have to be paid for. But when lay people help in this way, they are acting not as governors or parents or PTA members, but as 'friends of the school'. This distinction is as important for governors who hear pupils reading, or who give them mock interviews, as it is for those digging a swimming pool or advising on a legal contract. It must be evident to staff and governors. Role confusion is endemic in schools, most commonly so in small community schools. This is one area where it must not arise, or the role of the governing body is compromised in its legal status and its strategic role.

EXAMPLES OF TARGETS FOR THE SCHOOL ENVIRONMENT

Input Targets

- Policies for the environment will focus on fitness for purpose of delivering the curriculum.
- The resources provided by the school will be the most appropriate for delivering the curriculum within the budget available.
- The ethos and culture of the school is evident throughout the environment.
- The governing body will have in place a long-term plan for the development of the buildings and grounds agreed with the school's funding agency.
- The governing body will have in place a five-year maintenance plan for the improvement of the environment in line with its overall strategic plan.
- The unit expenditure per pupil on premises maintenance will be between £x and £y.
- The unit expenditure per pupil on other premises related costs will be between £x and £y.
- The unit expenditure per pupil on total premises costs will be between £x and £y.
- The unit expenditure per square metre on premises maintenance costs will be between £x and £y.
- The unit expenditure per square metre on other premises related costs will be between £x and £y.
- The unit expenditure per square metre on total premises costs will be between £x and £y.
- The governing body will receive annually a detailed report on the current condition of the buildings and grounds, including a room/curriculum analysis.
- The governing body will protect the health of all employees, pupils and visitors.
- The governing body will consider the health and safety implications of all school activities.
- The governing body will designate a committee (or individual) on the governing body responsible for liaising and reporting on health and safety matters.
- The governing body will have a policy on health and safety meeting statutory requirements (where appropriate,

the LEA policy will be supplemented by a statement of organization), monitor its implementation and evaluate its effectiveness.

- The governing body will ensure that the policy is drawn to the attention of all staff.
- The school will have clear procedures for identifying and controlling health and safety risks, and for reporting and dealing with irregularities.
- There will be codes of practice for staff and pupils for the use of classrooms, general use areas and specialist areas, which will be shared with them, monitored and evaluated.
- There will be adequate procedures for first aid in the event of accident and illness.
- Certificates of inspection of equipment and resources will be maintained according to statutory and local requirements where appropriate.
- Outdoor equipment will be checked on a regular basis for safety by the appropriate body.
- The school will meet (or exceed) required standards and current codes of practice regarding escape in the event of fire.
- Appropriate detailed guidance on health and safety issues regarding the buildings, grounds, fixtures and fittings will be provided in the staff handbook for all staff, and in guidance notes for temporary staff.
- Appropriate detailed guidance on health and safety issues regarding the buildings, grounds, fixtures and fittings will be provided in the handbook for pupils and parents.
- All seating will be appropriately sized and safe for its users.
- Any vehicles used by school pupils or staff in the pursuit of their work will be checked for safety, and all relevant documents will be available for inspection by the appropriate committee or individual.
- All staff driving pupils will have appropriate qualifications for the vehicle.
- The costs of breakages and vandalism will be monitored on a . . . ly basis by the Environment Committee.
- The Environment Committee will agree and monitor a policy on the conservation of energy within the buildings and grounds.

- The governing body will receive an annual report on the fuel costs per pupil.
- The school has a policy for community use of the premises, allowing subsidized use by local, voluntary and low-income organizations.
- Appropriate detailed guidance on health and safety issues regarding the buildings, grounds, fixtures and fittings will be provided in the handbook for all users, and displayed in appropriate places around the building.

Process Targets

- The premises will be inspected by senior staff at intervals of . . . weeks, with particular regard to the following areas: . . .
- The siting and proper functioning of fire-fighting equipment will be checked every . . . weeks.
- Health and safety training in the use of the buildings, grounds, fixtures and fittings is provided for all staff (details).
- Health and safety training in the use of the buildings, grounds, fixtures and fittings is provided for all pupils (details).
- Movements around the building are conducted in appropriate ways which enhance health and safety and the working atmosphere of the school.
- There is a daytime security system for the supervision of all visitors to the site.
- Within the context of a secure environment, visitors will be able to gain access to the premises and the buildings easily. For example, the telephone number will be easy to locate; the building will be easy to find; the entry to the premises will be clearly signed and attractive; the reception area will be easy to find.
- Visitors will feel welcome to the building. For example, the telephone will be answered in a professional but friendly style; there will always be an adult on duty in reception, or there will be clear signs as to how to find them; the arrival of visitors is welcomed; staff are pleased to see parents visiting; appointments with staff can be easily made and are not always necessary.
- The physical appearance is pleasing: the school entrance is clean and tidy; the reception area has attractive displays; visible staff are neat in appearance; the school is well

decorated; furniture and fittings are appropriate to adult visitors.

- The school gives off appropriate sounds: Appropriate languages and registers are spoken; 'sounds off' are appropriate positive and working sounds; all people address each other appropriately; there is a friendly formula for addressing visitors.
- There is appropriate community use of the premises in and out of school hours.
- Neighbours of the school will be consulted on any school matters that are likely to affect them.
- There is a clear and accessible complaints process for pupils and adults applying to every function of the school.
- Outdoor areas are checked daily for safety hazards.
- Waste bins in the school and grounds will be checked and emptied after every break during the school day.
- Toilets will be inspected and restocked after every break during the school day.
- Toilets will be inspected by a member of staff in the course of each break during the school day.
- Showers, footbaths and toilets will be inspected (regularly) for cleanliness and suitability.
- There will be appropriate arrangements for the storage, administration and recording of medication.
- There will be adequate provision and siting of appropriate first aid kits and facilities.
- There will be clean and suitable arrangements for the consumption of food.
- There will be suitable disposal arrangements for waste within the dining area and those parts of the school grounds to which pupils have access.
- There will be appropriate arrangements for the supervision of preparation areas and compliance with necessary regulations.
- The school will be generally clean, with surfaces and floors regularly cleaned.
- There will be appropriate safe drinking water facilities.
- There will be a suitable quiet area for the isolation of sick pupils.

Output Targets

- Pupils, staff and visitors will feel welcomed to the site and will understand what is expected of them.
- Pupils, staff and visitors will feel safe and secure on the site.
- Access to (all/appropriate parts) of the premises will be open to people with impaired mobility.
- All toilets will be suitable for the use of pupils, staff and visitors at all times.
- Pupils and staff will feel safe from adults and young people intending them harm.
- Pupils and staff will move safely and easily about the school site.

Outcome Targets

- Pupils and visitors will be stimulated by the school environment to work and/or behave appropriately.
- Pupils will develop a sense of ownership over the school environment, encouraging appropriate and progressive usage.

Chapter 6

Target-setting in School Personnel

Who Are the Personnel?

The governing body is likely to be the employer, or effectively the employer, of all staff on the school site. For the purposes of this chapter, 'personnel' will refer to paid and volunteer staff of the school. Pupils — included in the brief of some personnel committees — are actually the focus of every part of the governing body's work, and that is reflected in the way this book is structured. Relationships with parents and other members of the community are also considered throughout, and particularly in chapter 8.

Personnel are in every sense the most valuable resource of a school, answering for 80 to 90 per cent or more of the budget. In this chapter we are considering the governance of teaching and support staff. The former includes part-time, temporary, supply and visiting or peripatetic teachers. The latter includes classroom assistants (paid and voluntary), science, craft, design and technology technicians, office staff, supervisors for lunchtimes and other breaks and premises staff. It also includes staff who may be providing services that have been contracted out, such as meals service staff and cleaners. All of these will be members of the school team. Consideration will also be given to visiting workers — employees of the LEA and other consultants, traffic controllers, building and maintenance contractors, people who deliver to the school site. All of these are part of the school community, if only temporarily. The school owes them all a duty of care, and owes its staff and pupils protection from any risks they may carry with them. All of them need to be aware of, and reflect, the ethos of the school.

The potential for conflict is great if this is not the case. Many headteachers will spend an inordinate amount of time listening to the caretaker and cleaners complaining about rubbish and disorder, dealing with the inappropriate behaviour of visiting workers to or in front of the pupils, mediating between the teaching staff and the on-site youth club leader, consoling teachers who are looking for unequivocal 'discipline' from the top, chivvying education welfare staff, placating local inspectors. It might be instructive for senior staff to share with the governing body a log showing the proportion of time spent dealing with problems created by pupils, compared to the time spent dealing with problems created by staff. Headteachers have often (jokingly?) said that the school would run smoothly if it weren't for the kids. Perhaps, if given the choice between adults and children, they would happily plump for the kids.

Part of the problem here may be that, while considerable effort is put into creating a feeling of collegiality among the pupils — constructing an organizational image, holding assemblies, setting 'rules' and contracts on behaviour — much less time is given to inducting staff into the norms and values of the school.

Why Staff Matter

In 1994, a small-scale piece of research was conducted among leading businesses such as manufacturers and banks in the United States. The research concerned the reasons why business customers changed their suppliers. While it would be dangerous to extrapolate too widely from a meticulous but small-scale American study of business to the British schools system, the conclusions are worth the consideration of governors as employers (or as effective employers). The study is interesting because its results are, at first sight, surprising. On reflection, however, and compared to our own private experience of suppliers, it makes sense. Of the customers who had changed their supplier, 15 per cent did so because they had found a cheaper product elsewhere. A further 15 per cent had found a better product elsewhere. However, 49 per cent changed suppliers because they found contact with the old suppliers' personnel 'poor in quality'. The remainder changed because of 'lack of attention' from the supplier (reported in *The Independent on Sunday*, 8 January 1995). The conclusion must be that users of services are most likely — by a very long way — to make final judgments on the attentiveness of the people who represent the company. Nothing could emphasize more clearly that an organization *is* its people.

While the school budget represents this overriding importance of people, it is rarely reflected in the way a governing body does its business. How often do governors discuss the way things should be done in the school? How important to parents' choice of school is the way that teachers and reception staff treat them? How much of their confidence in a school is created by their interaction with those staff? And where parents have no choice of school, as so many don't, how much more important is it for the staff to offer them the precious commodity of attentiveness. Many schools, and many teachers, were brought up in a system akin to the service industry in a former communist state. Staff could get away with appalling service and inattentiveness because they were guaranteed a job and customers had no alternatives. Teachers have not been guaranteed jobs for some years, but there is still little or no choice for large numbers of parents and pupils. Schools have only recently begun to live with the idea that some parents (and usually those most in demand by schools) will vote with their feet. More likely, judgments are made about schools on, as we have seen, false premises and in a punitive way. But governing bodies need to know why parents have chosen their school when a choice has been available — and why those disappearing parents haven't. How much of it will be down to 'performance'? And how much to 'how we and our children are treated'?

The Governing Body's Responsibilities

The following areas need consideration and school policies:

Recruitment
Equal opportunities
Staffing structure
Identification of a vacancy
Advertising
Selection and appointment procedure
References (giving and receiving)

Support and development
Conditions of employment, including:
Equal opportunities
Appraisal
Staff development
Turnover and career routes
School-based and in-service training
Absence
Sickness
Stress
Health and safety
Job descriptions
Staff conduct
Pay
Competence procedure
Discipline
Grievance

Resolution
Redundancy
Retirement
Dismissal

Consultation
Consultation structures, including planning policy
Meetings
Relationships with professional associations/trade unions
Teacher governors

EXAMPLES OF TARGETS FOR THE SCHOOL PERSONNEL

Input Targets

- The proportion of the budget spent on teaching staff salaries will not exceed X per cent.
- The proportion of the budget spent on support staff salaries will not exceed X per cent.
- The proportion of the teaching staff budget spent on supply teaching will not exceed X per cent.
- The average contact time for full-time teaching staff will be . . . per cent. Contact time will be no higher than . . . per cent and no lower than . . . per cent.
- The extra non-contact time given to teachers with extra responsibilities will be . . . per cent (according to the responsibility).
- The contact time for senior staff (head and deputy) will be no less than . . . per cent. Senior staff will be available to cover for absent colleagues, and will spend no less than . . . per cent, and no more than . . . per cent of school-time on management/administrative tasks.
- The overall teacher–pupil ratio will be no greater than . . . and no less than. . . .
- A policy for staff development will ensure that all staff who wish to will be able to leave the school better qualified in experience and/or formal qualifications than when they arrived.
- A sum proportionate to X per cent of the staffing budget will be put aside each year to support staff wanting to pursue further qualifications.
- The administrator hours per pupil per annum will be not less than X and not more than Y.
- The governing body will ensure that the headteacher is provided with the support necessary to enable her/him to meet the National Standards for Headteachers.
- The governing body will ensure that subject leaders are provided with the support necessary to enable them to meet the National Standards for Subject Leaders.
- The governing body will ensure that the Special Needs Coordinator is provided with the support necessary to enable her/him to meet the National Standards for Special Educational Needs Coordinator.

- The governing body will ensure that all teachers are provided with the support necessary to enable them to continue to meet the National Standards for Qualified Teacher Status (TTA, 1998).
- A health and safety policy which will protect the health of employees, pupils and visitors to the school will be implemented in consultation with staff. The policy will identify the organization for implementing the policy, describe how it is to be implemented, describe arrangements for telling staff about the policy, specify how health and safety performance will be monitored and reviewed, and commit senior managers to reviewing and developing the policy. (Health and Safety Commission, 1995).
- There will be adequate procedures for first aid in the event of accident and illness.
- The governing body or its representative(s) will consider the health and safety implications of all school activities, policies and procedures.
- There will be a committee (or individual) on the governing body responsible for liaising and reporting on health and safety matters.
- There will be a policy for the promotion of good health in the school.
- The governing body will implement policies to regulate smoking, alcohol and drugs on school premises.
- The governing body will implement a policy on the management of stress within the workplace.
- The governing body will implement an appointment and selection procedure which will provide, by the selection of staff, the best possible learning environment for the pupils within the resources available; ensure that all appointments comply with education and employment legislation and equality of opportunity; ensure that the arrangements for recruiting and appointing staff offer applicants the best opportunity to demonstrate their ability to perform the advertised post.
- The governing body will implement a policy on the provision and receipt of references which ensures that candidates for posts at the school are evaluated fairly and openly, and staff of the school applying for posts elsewhere have the contents of references about them shared with them.

Process Targets
- Staff attitudes and morale will be measured annually by anonymous questionnaire constructed in consultation with staff representatives. Results will be shared with the staff, and action taken to deal with any areas of concern.
- An appraisal scheme will be implemented in consultation with staff, which will meet statutory and local requirements. Its purpose will be to identify training and development needs, and it will not be connected in any way with any competence or disciplinary procedures, or with performance-related pay.
- X per cent of staff at any one time will be undertaking some form of further professional and personal development.
- The annual turnover of teaching staff will be between x per cent and y per cent of the total over a five-year period.
- The majority of departing staff will leave for promoted posts or some other advancement in their careers.
- Staff will lose no more than x per cent of any non-contact time each month to cover for absent colleagues.

Output Targets
- The school staff will comprise, where possible, representative numbers of men and women in senior roles, and a cross-section of age, gender and ethnic profiles.
- Staff absence other than on professional business will not exceed x per cent in the autumn term, y per cent in the spring term, and z per cent in the summer term.
- The number of accidents recorded by staff on premises will decrease each year for the next five years.
- The proportion of staff training needs to be met that are identified through the formal appraisal process will be not less than x per cent.

Outcome Targets
- The school will offer effective and efficient deployment of all staff.
- All management and administration tasks will be directed at achieving the most effective learning environment for pupils.
- Teaching staff will display professional and curricular expertise; class management and teaching skills; quality of

relationships; commitment and professional attitudes (Statistical Information Service, 1988).

- Staff will leave the school better qualified than when they entered.
- Staff will gain a sense of satisfaction from their work.
- Staff will feel a sense of collegiality within the school.
- Staff will offer a balance of challenge and support to the school and its everyday practices and procedures.

Chapter 7

Target-setting in School Finance

More Change

Local management of schools became 'devolved funding' in April 1999, in another of those changes that makes the publishing of books on education such a hazardous practice. This will increase the range of services for which governing bodies have direct responsibility. School budgets will now include amounts for building repairs and maintenance, school meals, financial services (payroll, financial advice and information, cash management and banking services), personnel/human resources services (recruitment, personnel issues, disciplinary matters and legal advice), cleaning and catering, curriculum advisory and training services, school library services and supply cover. Of course, many authorities have already devolved some or most of these services; grant-maintained schools already had these items in their budgets; and LEAs will continue to offer the services on a buy-back system. Some schools will notice little difference in practice.

Nevertheless, the only functions remaining in statute to LEAs are strategic management (planning of the overall service), transport, admissions, special educational needs and the overriding issue of school improvement (DfEE, 1998c). The advent of the private finance initiative, where businesses are invited to provide premises and attached services to schools, offers the prospect of some governing bodies contracting out their responsibilities for the school environment and its management. In two LEAs, at the time of writing, private businesses are involved in the management of schools in difficulties. These innovations mark a significant change in the role of the headteacher, and in how headteachers measure their own success.

How Headteachers Feel about the Budget

In the 1980s, it would have been difficult to find many headteachers who prided themselves on their financial management. The school's financial responsibilities were confined to the capitation fund, an amount calculated by the LEA on the number of pupils in the school, to provide teaching and learning resources. Schools with good financial sense developed a formula for the distribution of this money to departments or classes based on the pupil hours taught. Perhaps they retained a proportion for whole-school or cross-curricular work, or for distribution by departmental bidding for long-term projects. By no means did all schools do this, and many operated in an *ad hoc* way, favouring some areas of the school work over others. This haphazardness was sometimes replicated at LEA level, where inspectors and officers might have funds of their own to give to favoured schools for pet projects. Headteachers could blame an unpredictable system for their own lack of strategic planning.

Their own self-esteem tended to be tied almost exclusively to the quality of teaching and behaviour management, although even here they could disclaim some responsibility. The teaching force was determined by the LEA, who made it difficult if not impossible to act against teacher incompetence. With school structures and admissions firmly in the hands of the LEA, even the achievements of the pupils, it could be argued, were beyond the control of the headteacher and governing body. A school's reputation, therefore, might depend very largely on the (observed) behaviour of the pupils.

It is, however, far more common now to find that headteachers invest an important part of their professional status in efficient financial management, alongside pupil attainment — whereas they may still shuffle off responsibility for, say, the school environment.

The Budget that Diverts Governors

Given the historical background, it was perhaps inevitable that the budget would absorb much of the energy of the new governing bodies in the early years of local management. They were not helped by the mystical processes adopted by many LEAs, or by the opacity of their schemes of delegation. In fact, local financial management (as it was called in its early days) may be partly to blame for the failure of governing bodies to adopt a strategic approach. Perhaps the then Department of Education and Science was to blame for not requiring LEAs to construct user-friendly schemes for presenting the budget to schools. Perhaps LEAs should take the responsibility for not doing it themselves; or headteachers, for diverting governing bodies onto financial matters where they could do 'less harm'; or governors themselves, because those confident and articulate lay governors who might have challenged some existing school practices felt more comfortable with financial matters. We can only guess. Perhaps it was more incompetence than political or professional conspiracy. But many governing bodies are still largely paralysed by an all-consuming passion for the mysteries of the budget. Here, they seem to say, unlike the curriculum, is an area where there must be tangible answers — if only we could find what they are. There's no slippery ideological nonsense about money.

How Financial Management Can Improve Schools

Actually, managing a budget *ought* to be one of the more straightforward jobs for which governors are responsible, if only information is presented to them in a digestible way. A governing body does not need an accountant or a bank manager to chair a finance committee — especially if they are of the breed that prefers to obfuscate their skills in order to make them seem more 'professional'. Rather it needs someone with the peculiar skills of unravelling the LEA's information and presenting it to the governing body in such a way that they can see, and choose between, priorities. Most of this, in an ideal world, will be done by a bursar or administration officer. Since the budget is the means by which the governing body's policies and priorities are implemented and its targets met, the staff should be left to get on with its management, following the guidelines laid down, and reporting regularly on progress.

The Finance Committee, therefore, may be *purely* a monitoring committee; although its members may sometimes help staff to construct the draft budget in the first place, and to lead the interrogation process in, from time to time, compiling a zero-based budget. Those finance committees that discarded budgets recommended by the LEA and dealt with a single lump sum to be distributed as *they* wanted, were those which enabled their governing bodies to get on with the proper business of planning, monitoring and evaluating.

School improvement can be enhanced by a governing body that has control over its finances. Evaluation is the key task which finance committees can enable. The concept of 'value for money' may be difficult to grasp in what is essentially a social service. But if desired processes, outputs and outcomes are explicit, it is a simple basis for budget management. Value for money requires clear success criteria for all expenditure, and so the previous chapters in this book may help towards it. What is especially important is that the governing body pinpoints developments which require extra expenditure — a new strategy for curriculum enrichment aiming to improve reading ages, for example; a project to improve attendance by appointing staff to chase up non-attenders; or increasing or renewing the school's information and communication technology. Each project is required to have a specific aim which may be expressed as a target, for example, improving average test results by a certain percentage; lowering the number of poor attenders; guaranteeing a certain number of hours for each pupil to work with a computer. Each project will therefore have a price tag, a desired outcome, and a stage at which it is agreed that the school has got its money's worth. Provided that the governing body has put together worthwhile and reasonable targets at sensible costs in the light of its statutory and curricular responsibilities, the issue of value for money can be dealt with as a straightforward cost/benefit exercise.

This approach to budget management focuses on the annual *changes* in totals given to budget heads and sub-heads, while the base budget is subjected to a thorough analysis every, say, three to five years. It can lead — as it has done in some schools — to a governing body dispensing entirely with the finance committee. Indeed, since a finance group must have its budget proposals decided by the whole governing body, and has no spending of its own to do, it is difficult to see why it ever needs to be a committee, rather than a standing working party. Working party status emphasizes its exploratory, interrogatory, monitoring and advisory role. The alternative danger is the emergence of the all-powerful 'policy and resources' committee of the governing body, the sort of body that emerged in local government by the introduction of corporate management techniques in the 1970s. Policy and resources committees can be tempting to 'businessy' governing bodies wanting to streamline decision-making, and can end up as classic and exclusive 'A teams'.

A finance working party can be invaluable, too, in overseeing financial benchmarking — checking school expenditure against local practice, using information supplied by the LEA, and against national patterns (using the Audit Commission, 1993, and onwards annually; National Audit Office, 1994; Funding Agency for Schools, 1997). This will allow the school to see where it deviates markedly from common practice, and to explore the reasons.

Resource management in schools has been under attack from Ofsted, with suggestions that, where resources are considered inadequate, it is more likely to be down to poor management in the schools themselves than any fundamental underfunding. It is something of a surprise, then, to read that HMCI considers financial control and administration to be 'good or very good' in nearly three-quarters of primary schools and to be 'generally sound and often good' in secondary schools (Ofsted, 1998a, p. 29 and p. 43). Similarly, most governing bodies are clearly meeting Ofsted's standards of financial planning, with about one in six primary and secondary schools showing weaknesses. By Ofsted criteria, fewer than one in 10 of all schools provide poor value for money, making inefficient use of staffing, accommodation and learning resources.

The budget itself, of course, can be seen as a set of input targets — the amounts the governing body guarantees to provide for each budget head (which may, like other targets elsewhere in the school need adjustment in the course of the year). It is then the task of the head and staff to meet these targets.

EXAMPLES OF TARGETS FOR SCHOOL FINANCE

Input Targets

- The gross cost per pupil will be between £x and £y.
- The teaching staff cost per pupil will be between £x and £y.
- The educational support staff cost per pupil will be between £x and £y.
- The administration and clerical staff cost per pupil will be between £x and £y.
- The midday supervision staff cost per pupil will be between £x and £y.
- The other staff cost per pupil will be between £x and £y.
- The books and equipment cost per pupil will be between £x and £y.
- The supplies and services cost per pupil will be between £x and £y.
- The repairs and maintenance cost per pupil will be between £x and £y.
- The fuel and light cost per pupil will be between £x and £y.
- The transport cost per pupil will be between £x and £y.
- The reprographics, stationery and telephone costs will be between £x and £y.
- The average cost per teacher will be between £x and £y.
- A formula will be agreed which distributes money to departments/subjects/classes allowing them to provide sufficient basic resources for the delivery of the school curriculum. An additional element of the resources budget will provide finances for which staff may bid for larger or longer-term projects.
- Between x per cent and y per cent of the total school budget will be delegated to committees of the governing body for spending decisions.
- Proportions of the total budget spent on the main budget heads will vary by no more than x per cent.

Process Targets

- Between x per cent and y per cent of the budget will be delegated to staff.
- Support and training in financial controls will be provided to all staff with spending powers.

- Expenditure on preparation for inspection, including notional costs of staff time, will not exceed £x.
- The headteacher/bursar/administration officer will report monthly to the finance working party and termly to the governing body on the current state of the budget.

Output Targets

- The expenditure out-turn will be within 5 per cent of the projected total.
- The budget will provide school resources fit for the purpose of delivering the curriculum.
- Budget reserves exceeding 5 per cent of the budget will be earmarked for specific and agreed projects.
- The budget will contain an element for contingencies of between x and y per cent.
- The element of the budget spent on administration will represent between x per cent and y per cent of the total budget.
- The cost of recruitment of staff, including notional costs of staff time, will be equivalent to between x per cent and y per cent of the salary attached to the post.
- Elements of the headteacher's and deputy headteacher's salary will be subject to criteria agreed by the governing body which will be process targets as direct outcomes of their work.

Outcome Targets

- The school will demonstrate annually to the parents that it provides value for money in all areas of its operation.
- The school will display effective and efficient management of its resources.
- The headteacher will report to the governing body any shortfall in provision over identified need.

Chapter 8

Target-setting for Schools and Parents

Governing bodies have a number of statutory responsibilities towards parents. These are primarily about the information they must give to parents in the school prospectus and the annual report. But their responsibility to parents goes far beyond the legislation. In their duty to raise standards, governors need to recognize that the involvement of parents in their children's learning is an essential requirement. All the research shows that children whose parents are actively involved in their learning, doing such things as openly supporting the school, encouraging attendance and completion of work, acknowledging the professional expertise of teachers — these children perform better by every measure used. The governors — not just parent governors — are in a unique position in that their perspective of the school — like the majority of parents — is predominantly a lay one. They alone in the school can see the school as parents see it.

However, governing bodies have a formidable task ahead of them, if they are to deal with the communication gap between schools and their communities. A Royal Society of Arts report (Bayliss, 1998) identifies a series of mismatches between schooling and society which may provide insurmountable obstacles to bringing closer together schools and 'ordinary people' with 'ordinary' experiences of life:

- What happens in schools is driven by what is specified in the curriculum and the way it is assessed. There is a mismatch between what happens now and the need to equip young people effectively to manage their lives in the twenty-first century.
- The school system assumes that what takes place in school is learning and that school is where children learn. There is a mismatch between this view and the reality.
- The organization of the school day and year reinforce the notion that education takes place in strictly-defined circumstances. There is a mismatch between this rigid pattern and the increasingly flexible world outside school.
- There is a growing mismatch between the tools used in schools and the tools of the real world, whether for work or leisure. The equipment in schools, in terms of ICT, and of pedagogy — teaching and learning methods — are looking distinctly old-fashioned by comparison with the world beyond. Schools are becoming the unfamiliar environment.

- There is a mismatch between the teaching and learning methods used in schools and the understanding scientists now have of the way the human brain works. Advances in scientific knowledge should be incorporated into the techniques used in schools.
- There is a mismatch between the move to flatter, less hierarchical structures in the business world and the traditional management structures of schools. Schools could learn from business experience.
- There is a mismatch between the policy emphasis placed on education and the availability of school facilities. The heavy public investment in physical facilities is grossly underused. The flexible school should be a centre of community learning. (Bayliss, 1998, pp. 3–9)

There are serious long-term implications here for governing bodies. But there are issues which need to be addressed in the shorter term, too. 'We will only succeed in what we are trying to achieve in school when parents understand and share our goals', claims one of the schools featured in one good practice guide (Capper et al, 1998, p. 25). But this sounds too much like the one-way traffic that has dominated school–community relations for more than 150 years (see, for example, Gann, 1998, chapter 9). Ofsted's own research has shown that parents do not share the education world's obsession with achievement (*TES*, 9 October 1998). But probably neither do most schools. Probably, both parents and teachers agree that children need to feel comfortable in school before they can start showing reliable and sustainable improvement, and that the drive for early results, while favouring some children, may disadvantage others in the long-term. Ironically, the revelation of Ofsted's parental survey happened in the same week that there was a slowing down of improvement in the end of Key Stage 2 SATs results in English, and a slight worsening in mathematics results. There was also a welcome from the teaching profession and from parents' organizations when the DfEE told infant schools to stop 'blackmailing' parents, that if they did not get their children into school at age 4, there might not be a place for them at age 5.

This apparent mismatch between what parents (and to a large extent teachers) want from schools, and what they are increasingly getting, may be making them more assertive. There is some evidence that parents want to be more involved in the strategic direction of schools, but that there are not enough ways into the system. They also want to see more involvement generally by non-governmental groups. For example, the majority of parents want to see more widespread consultation over the setting of schools' performance standards. In one survey, 77 per cent of parents thought they themselves should be consulted, 78 per cent thought classroom teachers should be consulted, 73 per cent school governors and 69 per cent school and education managers (Public Management Foundation, 1997, pp. 14–15). While legislation continues to provide a framework where consultation *can* happen, it fails to ensure that wider participation *does* happen. For example, an increase in the number of parent governors does not necessarily mean any increase in their effectiveness, which is heavily dependent on the prevailing school (and LEA) ethos. The requirement for governing bodies to develop home–school agreements does not protect parents from the kind of agreements that reflect only the *responsibilities* of parents and only the *rights* of schools — school–home agreements would be a more accurate name for these. For a better example, see figure 8.1.

Among the project schools featured in *Successful Schools* (Capper et al, 1998), mentioned above, the shared characteristic is a respect for parents' rights and a recognition of the schools' own responsibilities. They acknowledge that they are starting from a position where parents may distrust all organizations, all large institutions; parents whose experience of life is that society excludes them from decision-making and, indeed, from any significant power over their own and their children's lives. Their own experiences of schools may well have been negative, and they will expect that their experience as parents of schoolchildren will be pretty unrewarding too; a chapter of summonses to the school, of poor results critically reported to them, of blame and of failure. It is not only parents who may start on the back foot, in their relationship with schools. Teachers, too, will recognize that no-one has thought to prepare them for this vital aspect of their work: 'Sadly, we do not receive any initial training on interacting with parents, and some staff do not relish this important part of their role' (ibid, p. 25).

Governing bodies who claim that lack of parental involvement is due to apathy or to the fact that parents must be so happy with the school's performance that they just want to let it get on with it, must take their share of the responsibility for the failure of the 'partnership'. 'In order to understand . . . the gap that appears to exist between professional practice and parents' needs it is necessary to move beyond simplistic attributions of blame and look at the systemic and structural factors that impede communications', suggest Clark and Power (1998) in their study of school reports and parents' evenings (p. 52). Clark and Power indicate that these factors include professional concerns — expertise, the increasing demands on teachers' time, teachers' priorities in the institution, and social and cultural differences — which clash with the parents' overriding interest in the individual child.

That so many schools *do* succeed in involving their parents — especially in those communities where parents might have the surest grounds for lacking confidence in the system — shows that there are strategies which all governing bodies should consider. These include:

- parents' workshops, for example, in literacy (including helping children to read) and numeracy, information and communication technology, curriculum information, assessment and evaluation, understanding children's behaviour, English as a second language for parents with other first langauges, using the library, special educational needs, bullying, homework and study skills, parenting skills;
- attendance support;
- free transport and crèches at parents' meetings;

Figure 8.1 North Manchester High School for Girls: Partnership agreement between parent/student/school

	As parent(s) we/I will do our/my best to . . .	As a student I will do my best to . . .	As a school we will do our best to . . .
Being ready for school	send our/my daughter to school in full school uniform. make sure our/my daughter has the right equipment for school.	always wear full school uniform. bring the right equipment to school.	insist that school uniform is worn at all times. tell your daughter what she needs for lessons.
Attendance/ punctuality	make sure our/my daughter attends school on time every day.	attend school every day on time.	encourage good attendance and punctuality and to reward these.
Class and homework	take an interest in the work of our/my daughter. encourage our/my daughter to always do her best. make sure our/my daughter does her homework.	listen to my teacher and work hard. write all homework in my planner, do my homework and hand it in on time.	teach good lessons. prepare your daughter in a range of subjects that will allow her to succeed in national examinations. set appropriate work which will be marked regularly. provide a homework timetable and planner and to set homework.
Behaviour	encourage our/my daughter to have high standards of behaviour at all times.	behave well in and outside of school and follow the code of conduct.	encourage high standards of behaviour always.
Pastoral support	let the school know if there are any problems likely to affect our/my daughter's learning.	let my teacher know if I have any worries.	listen and respond quickly to any concerns.
Links with school	attend parents' evenings. read letters from school and reply if necessary. support the school if sanctions, for example, detentions become necessary.	take all letters home to parent(s). complete any sanctions, if necessary.	hold regular parents' evenings. report regularly on your daughter's progress, attendance and punctuality. inform you of any worries or concerns where necessary.
Extra-curricular/life of the school	support events that the school is involved in.	find out what opportunities are open to me.	inform you of any events that the school is involved in.

Parent's signature   Parent's signature   Date

Student's signature   Date

Signed on behalf of the school   Date

- homework club;
- staff visiting homes and local community groups;
- neighbourhood parents' evenings;
- community use of the premises;
- community learning/participation projects, for example, in arts and crafts;
- questionnaires/interview surveys/focus groups;
- newsletters;
- booklets and lessons concerning phase transitions;
- introductory video;
- INSET for whole staff and governors;
- clear statements of expectations of parents and their rights;
- clear statements of commitment of the school;
- some reflection of the range of communities in which parents live among teaching and other staff;
- consideration of the reasons why parents do not get involved, such as asking the following questions, suggested by Capper et al (1998), about parents who don't come to parents' evenings:
  — Do they have difficult working hours?
  — Are they unable to attend school events because of transport problems?
  — Do they have family circumstances (other children or elderly relatives to care for, for example) which might make it hard for them to get out of the home?
  — Do they have a disability which would make a journey to school difficult and movement around the school a problem or an embarrassment?
  — Do they have a 'mental block' about schools because they do not feel that their own education was particularly successful?
  — Are they afraid that the school might blame, humiliate or reject them?
  — Are there cultural barriers which might lead parents to think that it's not for them?
  — Are fathers deterred from coming into school because they see it as a predominantly female domain?
  — Have we considered alternative, non-traditional and non-stereotypical options for involving parents in the life of the school? (p. 39).

These are the sorts of issues which need to be considered in setting targets for the school in its development of a true partnership with parents. 'For some parents, notably working class parents and those with little or no English, school remains "another country" with its inscrutable professional discourse' (Clark and Power, 1998, p. 52).

EXAMPLES OF TARGETS FOR SCHOOLS IN THEIR RELATIONSHIP WITH PARENTS AND THE COMMUNITY

Input Targets

- A satisfaction questionnaire will be delivered to all parents once a year, covering areas such as learning outcomes, social aspects of the school, health, safety, confidence, enjoyment, values.
- Coopted governors will reflect the life of the local community.
- There will be a published complaints procedure which parents will be encouraged to use when appropriate.
- The governing body will exceed statutory requirements in the information it makes available to parents.
- The information given to parents will be appropriate, and presented in an appropriate format and language.
- There will be a clear published procedure for parents to gain quick access to staff.

Process Targets

- Where possible and appropriate, governing body planning and policy-making will take account of consultation with representative groups of parents.
- The Parent Teacher Association will meet x times each term.
- There will be x curriculum workshops for parents for each year group each year.
- Where appropriate, parents and other members of the community will be invited to participate in school activities, for example, parent/pupil reading schemes, classroom work, school trips (see Statistical Information Service, 1988).

Output Targets

- Requests for admissions and transfers from other schools will hold at between x and y per year. This figure will be reviewed annually in the light of changing circumstances in the community.
- Attendance at the Annual Parents Meeting will reach x by the year 2002.
- Attendance at Parents' Evenings will be between x and y per cent of pupils.

- The Parent Teacher Association will have an active membership of between x and y.

Outcome Targets
- Parents will feel a sense of ownership over the school.
- The community will protect the school.
- The use of school buildings will reflect the needs of the local community.

Chapter 9

How to Govern a School:
The Performance of the
Governing Body

The governing body is responsible for the performance of the school. It is also accountable to the community for the performance of the school. What does it have to be like to do these two jobs well?

Governing body self-review became a hot topic as the movement for school improvement gained pace. First, in a series of publications, including a White Paper, the new Labour government reasserted the central role of the governing body in promoting and enabling school effectiveness (DfEE, 1997a onwards). Secondly, Ofsted evaluations of governing bodies, though controversial for the rather hotchpotch way in which they were introduced and conducted for the spring term of 1998, allowed some judgments to be made by inspectors using a standard format. Thirdly, the new Code of Practice (DfEE, 1998a) emphasized the diminished ability of LEAs to intervene in schools that were running satisfactorily. Only when things were palpably going wrong could LEAs step in — not only because that was government policy, but also because they would no longer have the human resources to do anything more. This new model would be reinforced by the introduction of Ofsted inspections of LEAs. One element of such inspections was to be the effectiveness of the support that LEAs give to governors, so it was now very much in their interests to develop an overall view of how governing bodies perform.

LEAs set about developing a range of self-review exercises — although many continued to find it difficult to allow governors to decide for themselves whether or not such exercises were necessary. Such self-review tended, in many instances, to focus on the efficiency and, to a limited extent, the effectiveness of the governing body in doing its job — *how* it worked, rather than *what* it did. These followed models in earlier publications such as *Lessons in Teamwork* (Audit Commission/Ofsted, 1995). But efficiency and effectiveness are not the only desirable qualities of a governing body.

Professional educationists in schools and LEAs, and politicians in local and national government, are not the owners of the education service. They exercise custody over it, on the behalf of those people who use it and pay for it — the community. So *quis custodiet ipsos custodes?* Who guards the guards? That is the job of the governors.

A school which fails to deliver the goods (whatever the goods are by the latest government thinking) will have much closer custody exercised over it by its LEA. A similar relationship will operate at the school level — a school staff which fails to deliver according to what the governing body wants delivered, will be subjected to much closer scrutiny from its governors (remembering, of course, that they *include* the headteacher). Normally, the governing body will have in place fairly loose and generalized policies and procedures. Governors know that the school is doing what they want it to do, and that it is producing the results they want it to produce, by monitoring and evaluation. The governors 'control the inside by staying on the outside' (Carver, 1990). For example, governors 'lay down the broad principles underlying the whole school curriculum: its aims and objectives; its success criteria; arrangements for monitoring and evaluation' (Gann, 1998, p. 54). But where the staff are not doing what they should be doing, or where they are not producing the results that it wants, the governing body moves down to the next level of detail and intervention. It continues to move down as long as it needs. But as soon as its purposes are clear and its requirements are being met, it 'stops speaking'. If this point is not reached before it gets to the level of day-to-day management, which is the headteacher's province, then the governors have to take drastic action. This will include questioning the head and staff's ability to deliver, bringing in advisers from the LEA or elsewhere — and questioning its own practices. So, the extent of delegation and the staff's freedom to operate is dependent on its ability to deliver what the governing body wants it to deliver. So '*all* delegation to management is purposeful and intended, not by default' (ibid, p. 55).

The Governing Body's Authority

Deciding the aims of the school; deciding how the school should be run; agreeing the development plan; deciding how to spend the money; ensuring that the curriculum is being delivered; appointing staff; setting targets for the school — there's not much responsibility left for anyone but the governing body for the strategic direction of the school. The governors are, effectively, the owners of every policy and procedure that the school has — they are the owners of the expectations and aspirations of the school, too. While the headteacher remains the single most influential figure in the school, governing bodies are growing into their statutory responsibilities. There is an increasing correlation between the effective governing body and the successful school.

At the same time, we are seeing the increasing dictation of what a successful school is by the educational establishment — by the DfEE and its growing control over the activities of the school — the National Curriculum, the homework policy, literacy and numeracy strategies, the targets to be set, and so on.

Governing bodies and their headteachers have to determine what they want from their school, and what they want for their pupils. They have to do this assertively, or it will be done for them. Just as governing bodies have spent the last 10 years establishing themselves as the ultimate authority in and for the school, now they must join with the staff, the parents and the children to resist attempts by the DfEE, some LEAs, Ofsted, and the wider school effectiveness movement to set the agenda for all schools. An assertive governing body does not, then, take power away from the headteacher. On the contrary, in order that the governing body can give legitimacy to the headteacher's managerial leadership, the governors must take on board and exercise the range of duties which is theirs and theirs alone. It has to display a range of characteristics to do this so that the school continues to get better in the way that the governing body wants it to.

In the face of such formidable 'allies', the successful governing body must be:

- efficient
- effective
- democratic
- accountable
- open
- questioning

The Efficient Governing Body

The main tasks of a governing body are:

- *Planning:* This involves deciding the values of the school — expressed as aims, objectives, principles and targets. It therefore assumes that the governing body is responsible for devising and overseeing the policies and procedures by which the school puts these values into being. An efficient governing body will have a strategy for planning, so that it always follows the same broad procedure. The strategy will reflect the governing body's ownership of the school's policies and procedures, as in figure 9.1.
- *Monitoring:* Governing bodies use a variety of methods to ensure that the school is doing what it planned it should do. The main method is for the headteacher to tell them. Usually, this will be in the form of a report — the content of which is largely determined by the governors themselves. In consultation with the head, the information the governors need to know is given to them in an accessible format. In addition, governors will ask for reports from other teachers (for example, those responsible for subject areas or pastoral matters) and non-

Figure 9.1   A governing body planning strategy

The governing body agrees that all planning will follow these principles:

- Planning will be a joint exercise involving governors and staff.
- The plan will be drafted with a set of underlying principles laid down by the governing body or the appropriate committee.
- The governing body, or the appropriate committee, sets the planning process in motion.
- The plan will be presented to, and approved by, the governing body or appropriate committee.
- Where possible, the plan will be part of, and arise from, the school development plan.
- Where possible, the planning process will be consultative, involving parents, pupils and the wider community.
- There will be a named governor responsible for monitoring the plan.
- The plan will have an appropriate timescale attached for its production and approval.
- The plan will have clear, appropriate and measurable targets.
- The resource implications of the plan will be stated.

(Gann, 1998, p. 54)

teaching staff (for example, the bursar or finance officer, the caretaker or premises manager). They will visit the school — in a planned and negotiated way for explicit reasons; they will work on detailed matters in committees; they may be attached to a particular area of the school — a department or class or year group; and they will use question-naires to discover the impact of their policies and procedures on the day-to-day running of the school.

- *Evaluating:* Success — whether the school is achieving what it set out to achieve — will be defined according to the values the governing body has agreed. The targets or performance indicators or success criteria that the governors agree will, of course, take account of the statutory targets that the DfEE requires. But the efficient governing body will go far beyond these, using target-setting to identify what they mean by an effective school. Evaluation is then carried out against these criteria, to ensure that the school and its pupils are achieving what the governing body planned they should achieve.
- *Executive functions:* There are some executive functions that the governing body cannot — or has decided not to — delegate. These might include the recruitment and appointment of staff, and other em-ployment functions; managing the budget — with a clear concept of what is meant by 'value for money'; managing the premises; enabling inspection. The efficient governing body will have systems and struc-tures for these functions — clear committee processes and terms of refer-ence (see Arden, 1998), unambiguous delegation, effective reporting processes.

- *Communicating:* The efficient governing body will work effectively in a partnership with the LEA. The terms of this partnership are now laid out in the Code of Practice for school–LEA relations (DfEE, 1998). The governing body also has responsibilities to communicate with and report to parents. These include the annual report, with its ever-growing list of statutory inclusions, the annual meeting, the school prospectus, and the home–school contract.

The Effective Governing Body

To be effective, the governing body does its business well. It has clear systems of decision-making and conducts itself in such a way as to save time but ensure openness. It may use an evaluation instrument (such as in Audit Commission/Ofsted, 1995) to assure the quality of its performance. It has explored its effectiveness in teamwork — perhaps using Belbin's typology (Belbin, 1981). It provides roles for each governor, to ensure that each has individual responsibility. Apart from the Chair, Vice-chair and committee chairs, there will be governors with responsibilities for SEN, literacy, numeracy, training, induction, equal opportunities, health and safety, and so on. Governors will also be attached to individual subject areas or classes or other areas of the school's work.

An effective governing body will set a wide range of targets covering all areas of the school's work. The object of these will be to guarantee a quality education to all children. Targets will not just be threshold targets, as most DfEE targets are, but will enable and assure the attainment of *all* children. So they will take into account the *average* performance of children, and guarantee a minimum level of performance. Targets will be set not just on the outputs of education, as all statutory targets are, but on the inputs — the budget allocations, the environment, the ethos and values of the school; on the processes — the experiences the school guarantees to all children; and on the outcomes — the long-term consequences for all children and the community at large.

Indeed, the effective governing body will challenge the overriding dominance of the school effectiveness lobby, whose 'discourse of effective schooling and school improvement is narrow in its assessment of school effects, reducing school learning to discrete assessable and comparable fragments of academic knowledge' (Slee et al, 1998).

Such targets need not be expressed in the form that they are presented in this book. Indeed, schools will want to adopt their own language, which may reflect the needs of the parents as much as those of the governing body and the staff. Targets might be expressed as promises, or objectives, or as quality standards. Whatever language is used, the target will be something that the school considers to be important for the children to have done or to be able to do at some stage in their development.

The Democratic Governing Body

The democratic governing body ensures that it manages itself in a democratic way. It recognizes that all governors are equal, eschewing the development of A and B teams (see Sallis, 1995). It will enable governors to match up to Lord Brougham's axiom — 'to learn something about everything, and everything about something'. It will guarantee good practice in the way it conducts its affairs, having systems which ensure that group decisions genuinely reflect the governing body's priorities, and that delegated decisions are properly taken and open to scrutiny. It will have strategies that help it to operate as a learning organization itself — inducting new members, and using a variety of methods — beyond the formal meeting type — to develop governors' confidence, knowledge and skills.

In addition, it will reflect on its own 'representativeness'. Parent governors will explore ways in which they can represent all sections of the parent body. They will consider visiting cross-sections of families (or, in small schools, *all* parents), having stalls at school events, running their own newsletters (or having sections of the school's newsletters) to inform and consult. Teacher and staff governors will have formalized systems of consulting and informing their colleagues of governing body debates. Coopted governors will consider how they can represent the interests of the wider community. LEA and foundation governors will do likewise with their own appointing bodies.

The Accountable Governing Body

Democracy assumes accountability. Both Conservative and Labour governments have emphasized the duty of schools to be accountable not only to their parents, but also to their communities — whatever these might be. This implies that a governing body must never stereotype its parents or its community. It must operate a no-blame culture. Too many schools dismiss the poor attendance at parents' meetings as being down to the apathy, or to the satisfaction of its parents. An accountable governing body will always look to its own practices and those of the school first for the responsibility when its strategies fail to come up to expectations. Are schools discovering enough about the service they provide and what consumers — parents and children — and staff think of them?

The monitoring and evaluation process that schools engage in is often impervious to consumer satisfaction ratings. Yet there are many instruments around which will help governing bodies to develop accurate views of the public perception of the school. Some questionnaires have been developed with the aid of professional associations. Focus groups are another approach which schools can adapt from the world of politics. Auditing the school is a time-consuming, but essential process (see, for example, Waller and Waller, 1998). Perhaps surprisingly, then, primary schools are better at it than secondary schools.

Such consultation depends, for its effectiveness, on negotiating with all interested parties the content of the consultation — what do we want to know? Secondly, there must be an efficient communication system. Thirdly, all interested parties must be told of the outcomes. Fourthly, the governing body must take action, and report back on the effectiveness of the action.

Governing bodies must start from the question — what should *we* do to help others get more involved? How can we develop an equal partnership with parents and the community, not just in rhetoric, but in practice?

The Open Governing Body

Openness and accountability go hand in hand. Reporting systems must address the issues which really exercise parents and pupils, however uncomfortable these may be — bullying, drugs, even the quality of teaching! Schools have been very defensive in the past. They have relied on deference — in both internal (staff–staff and staff–pupil) and external (school–parent; school–LEA) relationships. They have traded on their compulsoriness and used the esoteric nature of teaching content and skills as a shield against 'ordinary people'. Governing bodies, comprising predominantly lay people, are the antidote to this, if they choose. They must avoid being 'incorporated' into the institution. They must maintain at least an arm's length from the school, so that they can play the part of the critical friend rather than, as Tim Brighouse, Chief Education Officer for Birmingham, has labelled some of them, 'uncritical lovers'.

This means that the governing body must look closely at the quality of its own, and the school's, communications. Are they sent in an appropriate way? Are they written in appropriate language? Do they take into account the parents' perspective — that is, their overriding concern for the welfare of their own child? Are reporting and consultation predominantly about the past — things the governing body has done — or are they concerned with decisions to be taken in the future — what they might do, given the support of the parents and pupils?

Are the governing body's decisions truly open to scrutiny, or are the statutory requirements of publication of agenda and minutes followed in merely a token form? Are parents, staff (and pupils) invited, even encouraged, to observe governing body meetings and join in on working parties and committees? Do the headteacher and staff actively encourage discussions and debates about controversial issues? Or do they represent themselves as the gatekeepers of knowledge and expertise?

Does the school have an effective and publicized complaints procedure? Are complaints recorded, categorized and reported to the governors? Do staff and governors regard complaints as a nuisance, to be discouraged; or as a gift from the user, to help them improve their practice? Is the number of complaints seen as being in negative or positive correlation with the effectiveness of the school? Perhaps, (within limits!) the more complaints we get, the more effective we are — because complainers recognize that we are an organization that acts on its feedback.

Openness about schools is a comparatively new phenomenon — HMI reports only began to be published in the early 1980s. Much of the information that schools now have to publish is linked with a culture of public shame — league tables, failing schools. If a school takes the initiative, and begins to talk and write openly about its 'secrets' (which almost everyone in the community knows anyway), honesty may begin to drive out fear.

The Questioning Governing Body

The term 'critical friend' has been overworked in describing the ideal relationship between governing body and school. Perhaps the questioning governing body is a more useful model. A Conservative government minister, speaking in 1996 (quoted in Gann, 1998) spoke of the relationship between the head and the governing body as a marriage. But it's an odd marriage where only one of the partners can institute divorce proceedings. The head has a dual role — as a full member of the governing body, and therefore sharing corporate responsibility for all its decisions — including those (s)he disagrees with — and as its chief executive and senior professional adviser.

Table 1.2 on page 11 suggests the questions that customers, non-executive directors and the managing director of a car garage might ask. Governors might explore the parallels. What are the questions that parents, governors and headteacher might ask of their school?

Since headteachers and governors share the responsibility for the direction and the effectiveness of their school — with the governing body carrying the ultimate legal authority for everything that happens in them — the question of joint training and development is critical. What training programme does the governing body have? Does it support them in doing the job? Does it give them the confidence, knowledge and skills to perform effectively?

Governing the Improving School

The new governing bodies are growing up. Some of this development can be expressed in terms of the level of maturity they have achieved since their birth in 1988. Certainly, there are governing bodies who are still childishly dependent upon the LEA — or perhaps the headteacher — as parent. These are not used to, or afraid of having to make, decisions. They are the 'supporters' clubs, standing on the terraces and cheering. More common is the governing body which is finding its feet. It has well-developed structures and plays a significant part in planning, monitoring and evaluating. But it is still not 'in charge'. Faced with the need to make important or urgent decisions, it funks it, and reverts to childishness — just like an adolescent, it sometimes makes no, or the dramatically wrong, decision. However, the governing body which has achieved

Table 9.1   Stages of development in governing bodies

AREA OF OPERATION	IMMATURE	ADOLESCENT	MATURE
Doing business	Subordinate to the LEA or to a dominant individual (usually the head)	Aware of legal responsibilities and generally participating in decisions	Individual functions shared out; a full partnership with staff
Planning	Development plan prepared by head (and staff) and presented for approval	Some governors participate with staff in development planning	All strategic planning starts and finishes in the governing body. Principles and procedures laid down by full governing body
Monitoring	Head is only and independent monitor	Some governors involved in monitoring; head reports to governing body on progress of its plans	Governing body has clear steps and timescales for achieving its objectives; staff & governors report on progress
Evaluating	DfEE criteria and targets only	Governors have some success criteria and targets	Governing body has clear success criteria and targets, and makes promises to parents and pupils
Finance	Dependent on one source; accepting external 'advice' on budget structure and content	Some independent decision-making; budget control exercised by a finance committee	Three-yearly or thereabouts zero-based budgeting; full participation by all governors in setting of priorities
Quality of service	Static	Some development of ideas	Quality of service a key notion
Staffing	Governors dependent on head (and other staff)	Some interchange of ideas, and some partnership	Staffing structure in place; governors and staff in partnership, with each given appropriate responsibilities
Employment	LEA terms and conditions or other statutory regulations only in place. Appointment process dominated by LEA or headteacher	Job descriptions and appraisal in place; some involvement in appointments by governors	Job descriptions regularly reviewed and negotiated; appraisal systems; staff development monitored and supported

the DfEE ideal of the 'critical friend' is a fully mature structure, recognizing its ultimate authority and capable of living with its mistakes. It regards highly, but does not exclusively rely on, its professional support. It recognizes and celebrates its achievements.

Miles of paper has been published over the last few years to help schools evaluate their performance. But the criteria used, while focusing rightly on pupil performance, have failed to take into account the whole range of the school's work. Inspections and league tables have focused on those elements of schools which can be measured, rather than starting from the question, 'What do we value in this school'? Such a question leads inevitably to a far deeper interrogation of the school's whole curriculum — assuming that the curriculum is everything that happens intentionally in the school. It leads on to the question, 'How do we evaluate the things that can't be counted?' One answer is by adopting a quality approach — an issue addressed in the final chapter of this book.

Below, the achievements to which a governing body may aspire are expressed not as targets but as a set of performance indicators, enabling it to evaluate its own effectiveness:

Figure 9.2   Performance indicators for a governing body

The Aim of the Governing Body
The governing body of xxxxx School aims for it to be a school where the complementary roles of governors and senior staff are not only well defined but are also evident through good, effective practice; the governors will be highly influential in setting aims and targets for the school, identifying financial or other priorities and in monitoring and evaluating progress towards meeting them. (adapted from *Ofsted School Profile requirements, Update 24*)

Performance Indicators for the Governing Body
Performance indicators can be developed around the key areas of governing body activity, for example:
1(a)   The aims of the school and the curriculum are clearly stated and reviewed annually.
  (b)   The values of the school are explicit and communicated to staff, pupils, parents and the wider community.
  (c)   All statutory policies and procedures and others as required are in place, and reflect the aims and values of the school.
  (d)   The school is provided with clear, challenging but achievable targets annually.
2(a)   The headteacher's reports provide information enabling the governing body to assess action in terms of its plans for the school.
  (b)   All governors participate in committee work.
  (c)   All governors have an attachment to one area of the school's activities.
  (d)   Governors adhere to an agreed policy on visiting the school.
  (e)   The governing body regularly uses systematic techniques to establish the attitudes of all stakeholders, including pupils, parents, staff and the wider community.
3(a)   The governing body receives regular reports on an agreed set of performance indicators covering all aspects of the school's work which focus on pupil achievement, or on areas of the school's work likely to affect achievement; the governing body receives regular reports on pupil attainment.
  (b)   The governing body each year sets mandatory targets for pupil attainment in line with statutory requirements, and receives regular reports on progress towards meeting them.

Figure 9.2   (Cont.)

(c)	The governing body each year sets a range of targets in pupil attainment and other areas of the school's work which reflect the governing body's aims and values, and receives regular reports on progress towards meeting them.
4(a)	The governing body has in place, and implements, policies and procedures for the recruitment, selection and employment of staff.
(b)	The governing body manages the school's finances within the budget accorded, and provides good value for money.
(c)	The governing body manages the premises in such a way that they are fit for the purpose of delivering the curriculum.
(d)	The governing body provides the appropriate information and support for local and national inspection to take place.
5(a)	The governing body works in cooperation with the local authority in delivering the best possible education for the pupils of the school.
(b)	The governing body provides the appropriate information to parents, as required by law and as it believes best advances the school's partnership with parents and pupils.

Performance indicators which can be tested by pupils, parents and others offer a transparent process of evaluation, contributed to by everyone who comes into contact with the school. They enhance a school's standing within the community by sharing its concerns, and by sharing out the responsibility for solving problems and meeting the challenges offered by new structures in education. So begins the process of handing back the institution of the school to its true ownership — the community that pays for it and provides its users.

Chapter 10

Quality Schools for Today and Tomorrow

The race is not always to the swift nor the victory to the strong; but that's the way to lay your money. (Damon Runyan)

What Is Quality?

Quality is a set of agreed criteria by which the performance of the school can be evaluated.

These criteria can be called 'targets' (although the word implies that they may not be met). They may appear as performance indicators, defining a quality standard. Whatever they are called, they are explicit statements of intent by the organization — promises of best performance. They aim to improve the service the school has to offer, and to provide a trail of accountability which users can follow when they are not met.

Quality standards can, in many instances, be quite closely measured. Others are deliberately less precise. This may be intentional, as some standards may be more impressionistic, about ethos or relationships, rather than statistics. With a set of more or less measurable standards, the school can be evaluated against clear and agreed criteria. This will enable any evaluator, internal or external:

(i)   to make judgments about the extent to which quality standards are regularly met;

(ii)   to make recommendations about action to be taken;

(iii)   to comment on the appropriateness and comprehensiveness of the standards, and make recommendations for amendments and additions.

The evaluator, then, has three main functions:

(i)   to confirm the governing body and staff in their regular monitoring of procedures (i.e. to ensure that what they say happens, happens);

(ii)   to make judgments about the extent to which the standards to which the organization is committed are achieved;

(iii)   to assess the relevance and appropriateness of the standards, and recommend changes or emendations to them.

Quality Service Standards

How, then, does an organization set about identifying the service standards to which it believes it should commit itself? One model, developed for use with the voluntary sector, considers a range of 'customer assessments' as 'components' of quality:

Figure 10.1   The components of quality

Reproduced by permission from Lawrie, 1995, p. 56

The governing body and staff would begin by looking at each of these components of quality, and deciding what standards they would set in each area. It should be emphasized that such an approach does not necessarily imply drastic change within the operation of a school. Many of the procedures incorporated into this model will be up and running as standard practice. What this does is two-fold. It organizes the procedures into a coherent structure; and it provides a model whereby a predominantly lay governing body without the professional background of the staff can evaluate the school's effectiveness. In each component, defined by Lawrie, the governors will find a series of questions to be asked, and procedures to adopt.

Information: 'The availability of information (in different forms) which explains the organization and the services in a simple way'.
  - Users (principally pupils and parents) are familiar with the history, structure and aims of the school.

- Information is given out according to what people want and need (rather than what the school thinks people should want and need).
- There is regular contact with users — written and verbal.
- There is a mechanism for publicizing the work of the school.
- All staff are aware of all the relevant structures and procedures, codes of conduct, development plans.
- All information is presented in the appropriate language(s).
- Information is presented in a variety of ways.
- Information is 'tested out' on users to see if it communicates effectively.

Reliability: 'The knowledge that a service will be carried out as agreed and to an agreed time'.
- There is a set of procedures which guarantees consistency of service, for example, assessment and reporting, code of conduct, health and safety.
- There is an explicit written agreement or contract between the school and individual users.
- There is internal and external monitoring and evaluation of the service.
- The organization seeks to improve its service by networking with other agencies.
- There is a complaints procedure which is used.
- User satisfaction is reviewed regularly.
- There are guidelines for response times to communications.

Competence and Accuracy: 'The staff have the required skill and knowledge to provide a service competently'.
- Staff are regularly appraised as a means of identifying areas of further development or training needed.
- Managers monitor by checking samples of work conducted by staff.
- Staff check regularly with users as to the relevance and accuracy of information.
- All staff receive a period of induction into the aims and procedures of the organization.
- All staff receive copies of all relevant procedures.
- All staff receive opportunities for training and development, both 'refresher' courses and in new skills.
- Staff are allocated a line manager, a support group and an experienced mentor.

Effective Access: 'The first point of contact with the school encourages the person to use the service, and the service feels "approachable". Also there is equality of access amongst users'.
- The school has an Equal Opportunities policy and procedures.
- The school has a complaints procedure.

- The school has a handbook for users describing the service, its monitoring and evaluation.
- All staff make positive efforts to welcome, and to listen to, users.
- There is no labelling of 'Troublesome Users'.
- Appointments are available with all appropriate staff at short notice.
- Reception areas and interview areas are welcoming.
- Space is available for confidential interviews.
- Relevant telephone numbers and addresses are easily available.
- Appropriate language and languages are used.
- Telephone and correspondence answering is welcoming and positive.
- The presentation of a positive view of the organization does not preclude or deny the raising of complaints and queries.

Effective Redress: 'When things go wrong or when a user feels that they have had poor service or unfair treatment they are able to have things put right quickly'.
- The school has a complaints procedure.
- The school has a handbook for users describing access to the service, its monitoring and evaluation.
- Users are encouraged to raise issues with staff at all levels of the service.
- Staff understand that complaints are material for improving service quality.
- There is a written contract between the school and its users, with a statement of users' rights.

Tangible Issues: 'The physical appearance of the service'.
- Premises used by the service are, and appear, 'fit for purpose'.
- Resources and equipment are appropriate and fit for purpose.
- All staff (particularly first contact staff) are aware of the importance of presentational issues.
- All written communications are presented in an appropriately professional manner.
- Premises and equipment are regularly evaluated by an external adviser.
- All staff regularly evaluate their working conditions.
- The premises budget gives due weight to the status of the user.
- There is a premises and equipment development plan.

Responsiveness: 'The willingness and ability of staff to provide a service in a personal and thoughtful way'.
- There is a code of conduct agreed and kept by staff and governors, and communicated to users.
- Every user has a member of staff who is the key or first contact person.

- Response times to communications are communicated to users and strictly adhered to by staff.
- Staff have regular opportunities to share issues about relationships with users.

Security and Safety: 'A freedom from danger, risk or accident. Personal security. Confidentiality.'
- A Health and Safety procedure is published, followed and regularly reviewed.
- Premises and equipment are fit for purpose.
- Users understand that their safety and security are priorities with staff.
- There are regular safety exercises (for example, fire drills).
- Users are exposed to an appropriate, acceptable and agreed level of risk in activities.
- Users are exposed to an appropriate, acceptable and agreed level of challenge in their own development.
- The differently appropriate levels of confidentiality in dealings between staff and users are agreed and understood.
- Written and computerized material is accessible only to appropriate staff.
- Users have a right to see any stored information about themselves.

Empathy: 'The degree to which staff listen to and explain things to individual users'.
- Staff are encouraged to act as advocates for the users for whom they are responsible.
- Staff training focuses on users' circumstances and needs.
- Users feel that the school 'sits alongside' them and gives them appropriate support.
- Evaluation of the service includes user perceptions.

Choice and Involvement: 'The ability of a user to influence the type and level of service provided'.
- Users are involved in or consulted on governing body decisions.
- There are opportunities for users to make choices at appropriate levels of the service.
- All users are informed of, and have explained to them, all the options open to them.
- The aims of the service are regularly reviewed with users.

Status of the User: 'The degree of respect given to the client. What does it feel like to be a user?'.
- The reciprocal nature of dependency between user and service is recognized by staff and users.

Figure 10.2   *Evaluating school empathy*

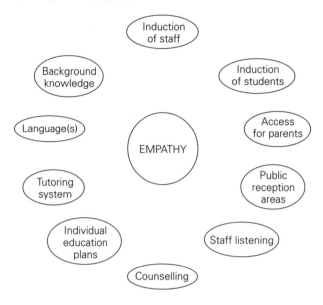

- ·Users are given priority (over, for example, other agencies) in access to staff.
- There is an agreed and evaluated written contract between the school and its users, with a statement of users' rights and entitlements.
- Staff training will focus on users' needs and rights.

The adoption of a model such as this will guarantee, as far as possible, that service focuses on a continual improvement in quality. Once quality standards are in place, they can, more or less accurately, be measured by an external or internal evaluator. The overarching question for the evaluator is: 'To what extent are the stated aims of the organization being achieved?'. An evaluator will produce a review of the service, followed by a series of action points to be addressed.

This approach can be scaled down to each particular quality component, taking into consideration the arenas of school activity which need to reflect that component. Figures 10.2 and 10.3 demonstrate how this can be done.

A Quality Employment Standard: Investors in People

Investors in People (IIP) is a national quality standard for employers, administered by Investors in People UK, which is administered and assessed through the local Training and Enterprise Councils (TECs) (Local Enterprise Companies in Scotland). IIP was launched in 1991, and focuses on the induction, training

Figure 10.3 *Monitoring school information*

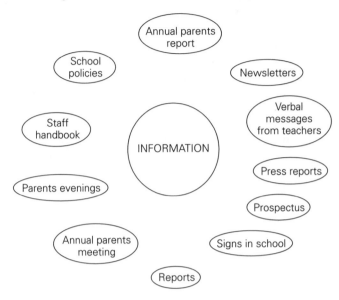

and development of staff throughout the organization. The standard is based on 24 indicators grouped in four principles:

Commitment: The employer makes a public commitment from the top to develop all employees to achieve its business objectives. This involves a written organization plan setting out goals and targets for all employees; and communicating the vision of where the organization is going.

Planning: The employer regularly reviews the training and development needs of all employees. Training resources must be clearly identified, and each employee agrees training and development needs with the management.

Action: The employer takes action to train and develop individuals on recruitment and throughout their employment. Action focuses on the training needs of new recruits, and the continual development of existing staff, encouraging them to contribute to identifying and meeting their own development needs.

Evaluation: An Investor in People employer evaluates the investment in training and development to assess achievement and improve future effectiveness.

Investment in training and its outcomes are regularly reviewed against goals and targets, leading to renewed commitment and target setting. (Investors in People, 1996).

In order to be recognized as an IIP employer, the school makes a commitment to its local TEC, producing an action plan to show where it falls short of the standard and how it intends to achieve it. TECs provide a 'toolkit' to assist in this process, including a set of questionnaires which can be used with staff to identify what their perception of the organization is, and its systems for supporting employees and volunteers. The action plan is usually put together with the help of an adviser, preferably one who has attended one of the recognized courses in IIP consultancy. When the TEC has received the commitment and approved the action plan, the school sets out to 'fill in the gaps'. Again, the support of a recognized adviser can be helpful throughout this process, which may take anything from six months to a number of years. When lead staff think it is ready, the school will return to the TEC a portfolio of written evidence demonstrating how each indicator is now met. Assessment is conducted by a recognized consultant appointed by the TEC, and is based initially on the portfolio, but more importantly on interviews conducted with a sample of all the staff and governors. The assessor then makes a recommendation to a panel appointed by the TEC, which makes the award of recognition as an Investors in People employer — or not. Organizations must show that they meet *all* the indicators to achieve recognition — there is no such thing as 'partial' recognition.

If the organization is committed to achieving the standard, the action plan will comfortably sit alongside, or within, the existing development plan, and the portfolio will be a collection of documents which form part of the school's built-in procedures.

Following recognition, IIP employers are reviewed every three years to ensure that they are maintaining the standard. Schools may receive some financial support from their local Training and Enterprise Council in paying for consultancy support. Small schools probably need such help, if collecting and presenting evidence, and maintaining supervision of progress, is not to become too onerous for staff. Larger organizations will appoint their own internal IIP lead officer — often a senior member of staff — to undertake this role. Schools that have achieved recogniton find that it 'unites the whole staff with a common goal'; that 'it puts the organization in the news'; that 'it really made me stop and think — to question what I was doing and why'. The process of gaining IIP can change the culture of a school, giving: 'a greater sense of unity and belonging among teaching and support staff'; it focuses on the 'central role of appraisal and target-setting through personal development plans, creating a stronger sense of worth and belonging, especially for support staff'; and is likely to result in a broader-based development plan (Lynch, 1996).

At the time of writing, there are 743 primary schools and 859 secondary schools recognized as Investors in People. A further 1330 primary and 1162 secondary schools are committed to achieving the standard (source: Investors in People UK, 1996). There are a number of advantages arising out of commitment to Investors in People, which will apply to other quality approaches.

The exercise requires the management and staff of the school to focus on the critical role of *all* the staff in delivering a quality service. The role of training and development — both in understanding the organization's aims and objectives, and in developing specific skills as needed — is subject to rigorous review and evaluation. IIP encourages the school to develop a procedure for identifying training needs, and evaluating the results of training, in a systematic way.

The exercise brings staff together for a common purpose. The sense of disparateness that is bound to invade the kind of school that employs relatively large numbers of part-time staff, and staff performing a wide range of support jobs, can be challenged by a new sense of collegiality and commitment; and the achievement of IIP recognition brings a heightened sense of self-esteem.

Other agencies, particularly funding agencies, will look upon a school's work with a renewed respect, once they learn that they are committed to IIP. It is perhaps inevitable that commercial organizations have looked down on the public sector in the past as, at worst, well-meaning amateurs in the provision of services. New accountabilities make this attitude unacceptable, but it may take a long time for perceptions to change.

Recognition also enhances a school's standing in the business and training networks of the area. Admission to this fairly exclusive 'club' can bring contact with local businesses dealing with a wide range of goods and services.

Finally, the benefits of 'tidying up' the procedures and policies that an organization accumulates cannot be overestimated. Managers in the public sector can feel overwhelmed by the structural long-term needs of an organization, alongside a reluctance to abandon the everyday short-term needs of administration and service provision. The opportunity that IIP offers, to sort out, update and prioritize, is invaluable after a period of rapid change and growth. It helps to put management 'back in charge', assists in identifying shifting priorities, and, generally, puts people back on task.

Naturally, IIP can consume enormous amounts of time, money and paperwork. The key questions to ask at the outset are — would we/should we be doing (most of) this anyway? What benefits will there be for the organization *apart from* the ultimate recognition? If these questions can be answered positively, and the resources of money and personnel can be found, commitment is justified (see Gann, 1996).

A Quality Institution

An effective governing body will recognize the importance of personnel, leading to a sense of collegiality; and the elements of quality leading to an agreed set of standards. Edward Sallis (1993) has suggested the differences between an ordinary institution and a quality institution:

Table 10.1   The quality institution

QUALITY INSTITUTION	ORDINARY INSTITUTION
Customer focused	Focused on internal needs
Focus on preventing problems	Focus on detecting problems
Invests in people	Is not systematic in its approach to staff development
Has a strategy for quality	Lacks a strategic quality vision
Treats complaints as an opportunity to learn	Treats complaints as a nuisance
Has defined the quality characteristics for all areas of the organization	Is vague about quality standards
Has a quality policy and plan	Has no quality plan
Senior management is leading quality	The management role is seen as one of control
The improvement process involves everybody	Only the management team is involved
A Quality Facilitator leads the improvement process	There is no Quality Facilitator
People are seen to create quality — creativity is encouraged	Procedures and rules are all important
Is clear about roles and responsibilities	Is vague about roles and responsibilities
Has clear evaluation strategies	Has no systematic evaluation strategy
Sees quality as a means to improve customer satisfaction	Sees quality as a means to cut costs
Plans long-term	Plans short-term
Quality is seen as part of the culture	Quality is seen as another and troublesome initiative
Is developing quality in line with its own strategic imperatives	Is examining quality to meet the demands of external agencies
Has a distinctive mission	Has no distinctive mission
Treats colleagues as customers	Has a hierarchical culture

Source: Sallis, 1993, p. 82.

There are, of course, other quality models. ISO9002 can be seen as a starting point (but not a substitute) for introducing what is called Total Quality Management. ISO9002 is primarily an industrial model and, while some schools have achieved it, it has been seen as a time-consuming and costly intrusion into service organizations.

For some years, the former Trustee Savings Bank (now Lloyds TSB) has sponsored school improvement through the European Foundation for Quality Management model of self-assessment. For governing bodies and schools interested in improvement through self-review, this is a comparatively cheap and effective alternative to some of the more complex models.

The key thing about quality management, of course, is not the award of a particular standard but the process an organization goes through in order to achieve continuous improvement. The quality standards discussed here are means by which a school can look at itself and the service it provides, with the aim of being able to guarantee or promise particular outcomes to its users, the pupils and parents.

The Nature of Schools as Organizations

One essential part of self-review — and an inevitable outcome — is that the school looks critically at its organizational structure. How tightly does the school control its staff? To what extent does it let staff use their own initiative and creativity? Handy and Aitken (1986) develop the notion of organizational culture modelled on the Greek pantheon. This notion is further developed in Handy (1995).

In the club culture, personified by the god Zeus, the organization is likely to be small and entrepreneurial. The dominant figure — usually the head — has inner circle control. Staff have immediate access to individual, ad hoc, speedy, but therefore risky decision-making. In such an organization, there is empathy, affinity, trust — or disaster. In the club culture, workers would be most likely, when asked what they do, to say 'I work for (the head's name)'.

In the role culture, personified by Apollo, the school has rational functions and sub-divisions. It is stable and predictable, with the human parts interchangeable. It is a safe culture, and therefore attractive to schools, especially large schools. Here, the worker would say, 'I work with (the school's name)'.

In the task culture (Athena), the organization is made up of self-contained units whose major task is likely to be problem-solving. Teams here are more important than leadership. Such organizations are fun, democratic — and expensive. They are rarely seen in education, as they are unlikely to be favoured by the inspection systems which demand systems and structures and consistency. In the task culture, workers would say, 'I am in teaching'.

Finally, Handy describes what may well be the more common organization of the future — the existential culture, personified by the god Dionysus. Such an organization is altogether more fluid; an organization which helps individuals to achieve their own purpose, such as a grouping of architects, barristers or doctors. It is primarily cooperative, with what management there is operating by consent. Workers here would say, 'I am a teacher'.

Changing Schools

Compare these cultures with Bayliss' mismatches in chapter 8. Consider the increasing demands of central government and the changing role of local authorities. Notice the increasingly assertive nature of governing bodies. How do the DfEE's strategies for school improvement — based on narrow definitions of 'success', and on an inspection system with a confused approach to quality assurance or quality control — fit in with the dominant trends in other, non-school, organizations? Not very comfortably, we have to conclude.

This book is predicated on the need for change in schools. But should schools collude with these centralized demands — demands which are largely insensitive to the customers — and ultimate paymasters — of education? Or should schools grow into organizations which focus on outcomes rather than outputs and structures, that serve the long-term and established needs of their immediate owners, the local community, rather than the short-term and temperamental needs of the political and professional hegemony. Such change as is required will overturn 150 years of schooling trapped within a model of production founded during the industrial revolution: Large institutions impervious to the needs — and the possible contributions — of individuals; organizations which receive and draw in and own individuals rather than reaching out to them; organizations subservient to an outdated concept of teaching and an archaic organizational culture.

Changing, as schools must change, into a sensitive culture responsive to need and in partnership with its users will certainly be a long drawn-out, and probably a painful, business. It is the job of the governing bodies, including the headteacher, to start the job that local and national government has flunked — developing a vision of what schools might look like, and what they ought to look like, in 20 years' time. The sooner we start, the better.

Bibliography

ARDEN, J. (1998) *Committees and Working Parties: Guidance for Governing Bodies of Schools*, London: London Diocesan Board for Schools.

AUDIT COMMISSION (1993 and annually) *Adding Up the Sums*, London: HMSO.

AUDIT COMMISSION/OFSTED (1995) *Lessons in Teamwork*, London: HMSO.

BARBER, M. (1996) *The National Curriculum: A Study in Policy*, Keele: Keele University Press.

BAYLISS, V. (1998) *Redefining Schooling: A Challenge to a Closed Society, Discussion Paper 6*, London: Royal Society of Arts.

BELBIN, R. (1981) *Management Teams*, London: Heinemann.

BOTTERY, M. (1992) *The Ethics of Educational Management*, London: Cassell.

CAPPER, L., DOWNES, P. and JENKINSON, D. (1998) *Successful Schools: Parental Involvement in Secondary Schools*, Coventry: Community Education Development Centre.

CARVER, J. (1990) *Boards that Make a Difference*, San Francisco, CA: Jossey-Bass.

CLARK, A. and POWER, S. (1998) *Could Do Better: School Reports and Parents' Evenings*, London: Research and Information on State Education Trust.

CONDUIT, E., BROOKS, R., BRAMLEY, G. and FLETCHER, C. (1995) *The Value of School Locations*, Wolverhampton: University of Wolverhampton Educational Research Unit.

DEMING, W. (1982) *Out of the Crisis*, Cambridge: Cambridge University Press.

DEPARTMENT FOR EDUCATION AND EMPLOYMENT (DfEE) (1996a) *Setting Targets to Raise Standards: A Survey of Good Practice*, London: HMSO.

DEPARTMENT FOR EDUCATION AND EMPLOYMENT (DfEE) (1996b) *Guidance on Good Governance*, London: HMSO.

DEPARTMENT FOR EDUCATION AND EMPLOYMENT (DfEE) (1997a) *Raising Standards for All: The Government's Legislative Plans*, London: HMSO.

DEPARTMENT FOR EDUCATION AND EMPLOYMENT (DfEE) (1997b) *From Targets to Action: Guidance to Support Effective Target-setting in Schools*, London: DfEE.

DEPARTMENT FOR EDUCATION AND EMPLOYMENT (DfEE) (1997c) *Setting Targets for Pupil Achievement: Guidance for Governors*, London: DfEE.

DEPARTMENT FOR EDUCATION AND EMPLOYMENT (DfEE) (1998a) *Code of Practice on LEA-School Relations: Draft for Consultation*, London: DfEE.

DEPARTMENT FOR EDUCATION AND EMPLOYMENT (DfEE) (1998b) *Announcement of Statutory Target-Setting in Schools*, letter from DfEE to schools, 20 May.

DEPARTMENT FOR EDUCATION AND EMPLOYMENT (DfEE) (1998c) *Fair Funding: Improving Delegation for Schools*, a consultation paper, London: DfEE.

DEPARTMENT FOR EDUCATION AND EMPLOYMENT (DfEE), QCA AND OFSTED (1997) *Targets for our Future*, London: DfEE.

DEWEY, J. (1938) *Experience and Education*, New York: Kappa Delta Pi.

EARLEY, P. and CREESE, M. (1998) *School Governing Bodies: Rationale, Roles and Reassessment*, Viewpoint No.8, September 1998, London: University of London Institute of Education.

FINDLAY, J. (1923) *The Children of England*, London: Methuen.

FITZ-GIBBON, C. (1996) *Monitoring Education: Indicators, Quality and Effectiveness*, London: Cassell.

FUNDING AGENCY FOR SCHOOLS (1997) *Cost and Performance Comparisons for Grant-Maintained Schools*, York: FAS.

GANN, N. (1996) *Managing Change in Voluntary Organizations*, Buckingham: Open University Press.

GANN, N. (1998) *Improving School Governance: How Better Governors Make Better Schools*, London: Falmer Press.

HAMILTON, D. (1998) 'The idols of the market place', in SLEE, R., WEINER, G. and TOMLINSON, S. (eds.) *School Effectiveness for Whom?: Challenges to the School Effectiveness and School Improvement Movements*, London: Falmer Press.

HANDY, C. (1995): *Gods of Management: The Changing Work of Organisations*, London: Arrow.

HANDY, C. and AITKEN, R. (1986) *Understanding Schools as Organizations*, London: Penguin.

HEALTH AND SAFETY COMMISSION (1995) *Managing Health and Safety in Schools*, London: HMSO.

HELLER, R. (1995) *The Naked Manager for the Nineties*, London: Little Brown and Company.

HOLMES, E. (1911) *What Is and What Might Be*, London: Constable.

HOPKINSON, D. (ed.) (1978) *Standards and the School Curriculum: Analysis and Suggestions from HM Inspectorate*, London: Ward Lock.

ILLICH, I. (1971) *Deschooling Society*, New York: Harper and Row.

INVESTORS IN PEOPLE UK. (1996) *The Revised Indicators*, London: Investors in People UK.

KAY, B. (1978) 'Monitoring pupils' performance', in HOPKINSON, D. (ed.) *Standards and the School Curriculum: Analysis and Suggestions from HM Inspectorate*, London: Ward Lock.

LAWRIE, A. (1992) *Managing Quality of Service*, London: Directory of Social Change.

LYNCH, K. (1996) *School Improvement: The Role of the Investors in People Standard*, Speech to the National Association of Grant Maintained Primary Schools, Stratford Upon Avon, 7 June.

MURGATROYD, S. and MORGAN, C. (1993) *Total Quality Management and the School*, Buckingham: Open University Press.

NATIONAL ADVISORY COUNCIL FOR EDUCATION AND TRAINING TARGETS (1998) *Fast Forward for Skills*, London: NACETT.

NATIONAL AUDIT OFFICE (1994) *Value for Money at Grant-Maintained Schools: A Review of Performance*, London: HMSO.

NEAVE, H. (1990) *The Deming Dimension*, New York: SPC Press USA.

OFSTED (1995) *Guidance on the Inspection of Secondary Schools*, London: HMSO.

OFSTED (1997) *Ofsted School Profile requirements, Update 24, December 1997*, London: Ofsted.

OFSTED (1998a) *The Annual Report of Her Majesty's Chief Inspector of Schools: Standards and Quality in Education 1996/97*, London: The Stationery Office.

OFSTED (1998b) *PANDA Report for 1997*, London: Ofsted.

OFSTED (1998c) *Secondary Education 1993–97: A Review of Secondary Schools in England*, London: Ofsted.

PUBLIC MANAGEMENT FOUNDATION (1997) *Hitting Local Targets: The Public Value of Public Services*, London: PMF.

PYKE, N. (1998) 'Failure label comes unstuck', *Times Educational Supplement*, 22 May.

SALLIS, E. (1993) *Total Quality Management in Education*, London: Kogan Page.

SALLIS, J. (1995) *School Governors: A Question and Answer Guide*, Oxford: Butterworth Heinemann.

SAMMONS, P., HILLMAN, J. and MORTIMORE, P. (1995) *Key Characteristics of Effective Schools: A Review of School Effectiveness Research*, London: Ofsted.

SCHEIN, E. (1985) *Organizational Culture and Leadership*, Reading, MA: Addison Wesley.

SCHOOL TEACHERS REVIEW BODY (1994) *Consultative Document: Performance Related Pay*, London: Office of Manpower Economics.

SLEE, R., WEINER, G. and TOMLINSON, S. (eds.) (1998) *School Effectiveness for Whom?: Challenges to the School Effectiveness and School Improvement Movements*, London: Falmer Press.

STATISTICAL INFORMATION SERVICE (1988) *Performance Indicators in Schools: A Consultation Document*, London: Chartered Institute of Public Finance and Accountancy.

STOLL, L. and FINK, D. (1996) *Changing Our Schools*, Buckingham: Open University Press.

TAYLOR, F. (1911) *Principles of Scientific Management*, London: Harper and Row.

TEACHER TRAINING AGENCY (1998) *National Standards for: Qualified Teacher Status; Subject Leaders; Special Educational Needs Co-ordinators; Headteachers*, Chelmsford: TTA.

WALLER, H. and WALLER, J. (1998) *Linking Home and School: Partnership in Practice in Primary Education*, London: David Fulton.

WALTERS, J. and RICHARDSON, C. (1997) *Governing Schools through Policy*, London: Lemos and Crane.

Index